TRICKS OF AN IRS CHEAT

And
Other Scandals You Should Know About Uncle Sam and Your Money!

Tricks of an IRS Cheat
And Other Scandals
You Should Know
About
Uncle Sam and
Your Money!

The story of the North
Carolina Kingpin of
Income Tax Fraud
as told to:
William Connor

A-Argus Better Book Publishers, LLC
North Carolina * New Jersey

Tricks of an IRS Cheat
And Other Scandals You Should Know About Uncle Sam and Your Money!

This is the story of the North Carolina Kingpin of Tax Cheats as told to: **William Connor**

For information:
A-Argus Better Book Publishers, Inc.
P O Box 914
Kernersville, NC 27285

www.a-argusbooks.com

ISBN: 0-9801555-2-5
ISBN: 978-0-9801555-2-5

Book Cover designed by Dubya
Printed in the United States of America

~Dedication~

This book is dedicated or perhaps consecrated to the millions of honest, hard-working, law-abiding, tax-paying American Citizens who are struggling under the onus of the tax burden. The same system that is aggravated by careless, ship-shod government workers and officials who believe there is no end to the amounts of money that can be sucked from the taxpayer; those that prey like a vampire sucking blood from its victims. And also by people like me that have been and still are using every technique, legal and illegal, to avoid as much of that yoke of tax burden as is possible.

~December 8, 2007 ~*~Bill Jackson, Tax Cheat

"You must pay taxes. But there is no law
that says you gotta leave a tip."
                ~Anonymous tax preparer~

~A Little-known Tax-Book Fact~

On December 7, 1941, two completely unrelated events took place. The most well known happening on that date was the infamous attack by Japan against the United States at Pearl Harbor.

The much less-known event was the publication of a book about income taxes written by a little-known comedian, Julius Marx—who was to become famous as—Groucho Marx.

It was unfortunate for Julius that the publisher chose to withdraw the book from distribution, deciding that it would be un-American to complain about taxes while we were being bombed.

Fortunately for us, that event led to Julius becoming the beloved comedian, Groucho; he of the mustache, bushy eyebrows, horn-rimmed glasses and the ever-present cigar,

Unfortunately, we didn't fare quite well with income   taxes.

~ Points to Ponder ~

~*~

"No government can exist without taxation. This money must necessarily be levied on the people; and the grand art consists of levying so as not to oppress."

~Frederick the Great, 18th Century Prussian king~

~*~

"The power of taxing people and their property is essential to the very existence of government."

~ James Madison, U.S. President~

~*~

"In general, the art of government consists in taking as much money as possible from one party of the citizens to give to the other. "

~Voltaire~ (1764)

"Kings ought to shear, not *skin* their sheep. "
~English poet Robert Herrick shortly
after the execution of Charles I, who had imposed
numerous burdensome taxes on his subjects. ~

~Introduction~

Nothing in the quiet, unassuming appearance of Bill Jackson would give an observer even the faintest hint that he is a proficient and confirmed income tax cheat. Standing several inches more than six feet tall, the balding, white-haired, portly Jackson resembles an elderly, successful business executive or a retired business owner considerably more than he appears to be a sophisticated income tax return manipulator who would try to twist the income tax laws to his advantage and to the advantage of his high-paying clients.

His easy-going, relaxed, "good-old country boy" manner is more reminiscent of Ben Matlock, Grandpa McCoy or Jed Clampett of television fame than of an accountant who pours ceaselessly over the gigantic myriad of complex and varied tax provisions in search of any small detail that could result in a decrease in the amount of his client's tax liability.

Yet, his slow, seemingly non-aggressive manner conceals a keen, razor-sharp mind that is filled with knowledge of obscure and little-known income tax provisions and he is constantly plotting ways to use those provisions, legally or illegally, to minimize the amount of taxes that his clients must pay.

In the United States, the "Law of the Land" is that the Internal Revenue Service is charged with collecting taxes imposed upon the public. In the performance of that duty, the Internal Revenue has been given virtually unlimited authority to enforce that collection as well as assuring that the taxed public remain faithful to obeying the thousands and thousands of rules and regulations that have been enacted by the Congress of the United States of America. The policing authority vested in the Internal Revenue Service to enforce the provisions of the Internal Revenue Code is truly awesome. No less impressive is the power to investigate and prosecute any person that seeks to circumvent those rules and regulations either for himself personally or by giving advice—even unpaid advice—to others.

To challenge that concept is to place oneself in direct confrontation; war with one of the most powerful organizations in existence: an organization that has virtually unlimited resources, money and manpower.

What could it be that would cause a reasonably intelligent man to willingly provide false information to this all-powerful Internal Revenue Service, one of the strongest and most vindictive departments of the Federal Government? An organization that not only can, but also will, most eagerly put such a person in prison? An organization that can, and will, destroy one's life, confiscate a person's property and put a person out on the street?

Why would anyone be willing to challenge a powerful, omnipotent organization that has the most sophisticated and complex computer system that has ever existed? An organization staffed with hundreds of thousands of attorneys and accountants? An organization that has composed a tax code that requires tens of thousands of pages just to print; a code that is so complex that not even the officials charged with administering the code can comprehend all of the complexities that are included in the millions of written words?

It is a given fact that the Internal Revenue Service is a huge, powerful part of the United States Government. It truly is the collection agency of the entire United States, and its powers are virtually unlimited. The agency and its employees are able to pry into any part of any citizen's life and affairs in its diligent search for the IRS cheat.

It is a fact that the agency has hundreds of thousands of employees and computers costing billions of dollars. It is also a fact that the purpose of those employees and those computers is to ascertain that Uncle Sam receives his full share of taxes levied against the United States citizens. It is another fact that the agency is responsible for collecting billions of dollars to fuel the ever-hungry monster of a government that has evolved over the past two and one-half centuries.

It is yet another fact that the Internal Revenue Service is the most feared, and without a doubt, the most despised agency of the United States Government.

Was it then personal hatred that caused Bill Jackson to become a tax cheat? Was it a disdain for the rules and regulations of the taxing agency? Did he do it solely for money? Did he become a cheat and help others avoid paying taxes because he felt that the Internal Revenue Service was unfairly taxing American citizens?

Perhaps one motive could be the enormous waste of dollars by the U.S. government. There will be a large number of these particular instances detailed in the pages that follow, although this is to be Bill's story and not just another frustrated author railing against an unfair tax. Could it be that Bill, like millions of American citizens, is fed up with the wasteful spending of the income taxes levied on the unwilling but helpless public?

Or, perhaps—and this may be closer to the true reason—he did it because the challenge was there; the sheer thrill and excitement of jousting with an ominously potent foe.

I've spent many hours and days over a long period of time in his company, interviewing Bill, yet I still can't determine his precise motive. Even after listening to Bill's story, the mystery remains. But, you decide for yourself. Is Bill just another crook out for all that he can get? Or is he, at heart, a rebel, not unlike the rebels that tamed this great land in the centuries past?

You will likely discover more from Bill himself as his story unfolds. You will learn of many legal and illegal ruses that Bill used on behalf of his clients, and other antics used by his associates or acquaintances in the income tax preparation field. He has been open and candid, holding nothing back and not trying to shirk his responsibility for the two separate occasions when the Internal Revenue Service was clearly the winner.

As you read of the techniques that were employed by Bill and his clients, you will discover that many, even most of them are both *legal and acceptable* to the Internal Revenue Service Auditors. That is, the procedures are legal **provided** that **all** of the rules are followed and that all of the information is *true*, *complete* and *accurate*.

Before adopting for your personal benefit any of the income tax reduction plans that you will learn while reading this narrative, be sure to check with a tax professional. There just may be some information the tax professional can give you that could keep you out of trouble. And, perhaps, out of jail.

From time to time, various quotes regarding taxes and the Internal Revenue Service will be inserted. The speakers of these words will be identified, should the source be known. One example is the "~ Points to Ponder ~" that led off. You may find these quotes to be humorous or ironic, perhaps even illuminating. The final chapter, "Just When You Thought the I.R.S. Couldn't Be Humorous" is a collection of quotes and jibes that Bill and I assembled while working on this manuscript. We wanted to include the collection for your amusement and we hope that you enjoy our efforts. We've had fun composing these pages and we hope you find our work to be entertaining.

Still, this is a true, non-fiction serious book.

Now, Bill Jackson's story in his own words and in his own manner without any attempt to edit either his language or his grammar. I ask my Editor and you, the Reader, to overlook lapses from proper grammar and incorrect English. Instead just relax, read, enjoy and be entertained, even mesmerized, as I was, by Bill's testimony.

~ Points to Ponder ~

~*~

"Where there is an income tax, the just man will pay more and the unjust less on the same amount of income."

~Plato~

~*~

"The greater the number of statutes, the greater of thieves and brigands."

~Lao-Tzu~

~*~

"Taxes must not take from individuals what rightfully belongs to individuals."

~Henry George~

~*~

"You cannot help the poor by destroying the rich. You cannot lift the wage earner by pulling down the wage payer."

---Abraham Lincoln

Chapter 1

So, you want to learn how to cheat on your income taxes, do you? Well, I certainly don't fault you for that. You've certainly come to the right place. But, beware of what you ask for; you might just get it.

Income taxes. Ugh! Pay taxes on what one earns? What an evil, vile thought! A legal "Rob The Rich and Give to The Poor" scheme that could only have been conceived by a sadistic madman. Or a politician. Never did Robin Hood have it so good. And the IRS goes him one better.

Doesn't it just gall you, having to pay income taxes on money you have earned while others, who know how and who are able to pay accountants like me, can avoid paying taxes altogether? Don't you think there must be a taxing procedure that would be less punitive?

And wasteful! My God! Did you know that the United States Government has spent seventy-four million dollars (That's *six* zeros, $74,000,000.00) of your tax dollars to promote democracy in Cuba? Cuba, of all places. Castro and all that. And, that among the 'vital' items needed for this purpose were leather coats, cashmere sweaters, a gas chain-saw, computer gaming equipment and software (including Nintendo Game Boys and Sony PlayStations), a mountain bike, crab meat and last, but not least, Godiva chocolates.

Duh!

Now, isn't that just too sweet?

Guess what, friends? It's your money they're spending. Or, at least, it was yours before the IRS took it away.

Still, let's be fair. Our government, as do all governments, does require funds for its operation. Nevertheless, there must be a better way and there certainly could be a lot less waste. Still, it *IS* the law—at least for now.

Many misguided protesters actually believe and contend that we are not required to pay income taxes. They contend that the levy is unconstitutional. Not so. It actually is quite legal. Robbery, perhaps, but it's still legal.

So, how did this highway robbery system known as income taxation and the formidable strong-arm collection agency named the Internal Revenue Service come about? Let's take a quick look at history.

Origin---The roots of the IRS go back to the Civil War when President Lincoln and Congress, in 1862, created the position of Commissioner of Internal Revenue and enacted an income tax to pay war expenses. The income tax was repealed 10 years later. Congress revived the income tax in 1894, but the Supreme Court ruled it unconstitutional the following year. But, that didn't stop Congress. There was "The Amendment."

16th Amendment ---In 1913, Wyoming ratified the 16th Amendment, providing the three-quarter majority of states necessary to amend the Constitution. The 16th Amendment gave Congress the authority to enact an income tax. That same year, the first Form 1040 appeared after Congress levied a 1

3

percent tax on net personal incomes above $3,000 with a 6 percent surtax on incomes of more than $500,000.

In 1918, during World War I, the top rate of the income tax rose to 77 percent to help finance the war effort. It dropped sharply in the post-war years, down to 24 percent in 1929, and rose again during the Depression. During World War II, Congress introduced payroll withholding and quarterly tax payments, and made tax collectors out of employers.

A New Name---In the 1950s, the agency was reorganized to replace a poorly operated patronage system with career, professional employees. The Bureau of Internal Revenue name was changed to the Internal Revenue Service. The IRS Commissioner and the Chief Counsel are selected by the president and confirmed by the Senate. The rest of the IRS is made up of career employees and civil servants.

Ah. Such a mild, innocent-sounding explanation. You might think Internal Revenue Service would have been formed to service the American Citizen. Far from that idea, but the Constitutional Amendment certainly did give the Congress the power to tax, and the politicians have been willingly – even joyously – taxing us-you and me-ever since. And, despite the many claims of tax reform and tax reduction made by politicians, the American taxpayers are now paying the highest amount of taxes in history. Do you believe that the rate may increase in the future?

You got that one right.

Having the opportunity to rethink the situation, perhaps we are being 'serviced'; if you are aware that the farmer has his cows 'serviced' by a bull.

There are two quotations that come immediately to mind.

4

"When more of the people's sustenance is extracted through the form of taxation than is necessary to meet the just obligations of a government...such extraction becomes ruthless extortion and a violation of the fundamental principles of a free government." ~Grover Cleveland, President, Second Annual Message, December 1886~

And

"Activities engaged in by a citizen to prevent the Government from confiscating the fruits of his labor are the noblest endeavors of mankind."

~Benjamin Franklin, Statesman~

With words from such learned men as Mr. Franklin and Mr. Cleveland, respected Statesmen, Politicians, Leaders and Spokesmen, echoing through one's brain like vivid bolts of brilliant lightning criss-crossing the ebony sky, how can one help but do one's best? Powerful words, aren't they?

But, "noblest endeavors?"

Really. Now, come on.

Of course, in all modesty, I'm not exactly that noble a person. Still, the statements are quite exciting, wouldn't you say?

Let's face the facts.

With the past, current and projected levels of waste and overspending, free giveaways and efforts of trying to bribe and influence the sovereign governments of foreign nations, it is impossible that

5

any sane person believe that our government is extracting only sufficient funds to meet its *just* obligations. Therefore the taxation—our taxation—has become *"ruthless extortion."*

Nonetheless, I will not claim that a great sense of chivalry played any significant part in my providing information and assistance to a variety of tax-filers as they sought to minimize the income taxes they would have to pay; that is, if they couldn't avoid paying taxes altogether

In fact, I will offer no defense of any kind. No excuse, no alibi. I did what I did and I did it with the full, complete and willing—even eagerly enthusiastic— cooperation of my happy tax clients.

And for a long time, I was quite successful

William has stated that the "~ Points to Ponder ~" have been included for your entertainment. For decades, the IRS has been the butt of jokes and comments, although you will find some of the points somewhat ironic. Even biting. Still, you may find many of the quotes, mostly from famous people, to be somewhat amusing.

Less amusing to you will be the "Do You Know.............?" articles that will be dropped in here and there. These articles are taken from the records of the United States General Accounting Office and the IRS that I studied during my research of the IRS for this book. When you look at the records, you will find out just how inefficient the Government is and just how much of YOUR money they are wasting.

And it is your money! You earned it. And they are taking it away from you! At least, the government is taking it away from some of you.

Of course, almost fifty percent of the population pays little or no taxes. These are the lower income people or the very wealthy. You will see how

6

the really rich actually pays almost zero taxes. Then consider that with the generous income tax breaks and the Earned Income Tax Credits, the majority of the lower income populace not only doesn't pay taxes, but is actually given cash grants. Sort of like a government welfare program, isn't it?

Guess who pays for all that?

You got that one right. Two for two.

And the Government doesn't even kiss you or say thank you.

Where's the romance?

~Points to Ponder~

~*~

"I think the complexity of our Tax Code is the worst problem facing our society...We wouldn't have either evasion or avoidance if we didn't have 10,000 pages of Tax Code it takes a machine to understand."
~Treasury Secretary Paul O'Neill, March 14, 2002~

~*~

"When men get in the habit of helping themselves to the property of others, they cannot easily be cured of it. The history of our Tax Code, in economic terms, mirrors the course of most addictions: advancing dependence, diminished returns, and deteriorating health of the afflicted."
~The New York Times editorial opposing the very first income tax, 1909~

~*~

"Taxing is an easy business."
~Edmund Burke in *Thoughts on the Cause of Present Discontent,* 1770~

.

.

Chapter 2

Did you know that the richest of the rich pays absolutely zero income taxes? Zilch. Nada. None.

True fact.

By investing their money in tax-exempt municipal bonds or other tax-free investments as well as investments outside the United States, the very rich are able to avoid paying any income tax at all, as all their income is therefore tax-exempt. Some wealthy people purchase tax credits from entities that do not fully use the tax credits they have earned. These credits are traded between companies and individuals, just as stocks are traded in the marketplace.

But, is that completely fair? Don't these actions place an additional burden on the low and moderate-income tax-filers?

Notice that I said 'tax-filers', not taxpayers. Actually, when it comes right down to it, the low-income population also pays zero taxes. Again, as bad as it sounds, this is completely true.

Not only is this a fact, but also many-almost all-of the lower-income tax-filers are sent a tax rebate check by the United States Government although there may have been no income taxes withheld. Through additional Congress-enacted credits such as Childcare Credits, Education Credits and Earned Income Tax Credits, almost fifty percent of our population pays no taxes. None at all.

Do you know what that means? It means the remaining 48 percent of the wage earners must pay the *entire* tax burden. Wow. Do you wonder that there might be a lot of resentment?

Along with the resentment comes a desire to find some way of reducing the tax burden, and many of those who have to carry the onus of the financial load often seek means to reduce the amount they pay. Even if some of those ways may be somewhat on the shady side.

At one time, my goal was to be the ultimate professional tax preparer. I wanted to learn as much about the tax program as possible. When I started to study the program, it didn't take long to realize that the income tax regulations are complex and difficult to interpret. Complex? Difficult? Make that read absolutely, completely incomprehensible.

Along about the same time, I began to realize that there could not possibly be a single human being anywhere that can accurately interpret the multitude of those regulations. Many of the many regulations are out-dated. A large number of those regulations conflict with other regulations within the same section of the Internal Revenue Code. This 'Code' is the 'Bible' under which the Internal Revenue Service is supposed to operate.

Okay! So if there is no single human capable of comprehending the entire Code, why can't someone— me, for example—simply say that the Code allows these deductions, or perhaps those expenses, or even these write-offs? After all, no one can say specifically that the actions in question are prohibited by the Code. And, if something isn't prohibited, isn't it allowed?

My decision has always been in the affirmative. Of course, I'm an optimist.

11

Well, if the average taxpayer wants to reduce his or her taxes, how can that taxpayer determine which deductions can be taken without incurring the wrath of the IRS auditors?

Simple. The taxpayer finds a willing tax preparer or an accountant that possesses sufficient knowledge of the Code to help the taxpayer in the preparation of his or her income tax return, using as many of the deductions as the taxpayer may find beneficial.

Such a tax preparer or accountant would have studied the Code in an attempt to find the obscure programs that will help taxpayer benefit from entries on the tax form, thereby paying less income tax.

Some tax preparers or accountants take short cuts and fabricate completely new means of maximizing deductions, while still others simply adapt or twist the language of the Code to benefit the taxpayer client.

How does a taxpayer so inclined find such an accountant or a tax preparer that is willing to skate on the edge, or perhaps just a little beyond? There are thousands of tax preparers and accountants vying for business, and most of them – especially the tax preparers – are willing to accept any information that the taxpayer client offers as being true and accurate.

That acceptance is especially easy; as the tax-filing client must sign a form that certifies the information he or she is providing is true, accurate and complete. The confirmation is given under the penalty of perjury.

Alas. From that point, it is a small, simple step for the preparer to help the taxpayer client generate the information, or expand upon it.

The tax preparer—absolutely proper in my opinion— must have the attitude that he or she does not work for the Internal Revenue Service. In fact, the tax preparer is employed by the taxpayer to prepare the income tax return utilizing his skills and the information available. The tax preparer is not an auditor and cannot be required to ascertain that the information is true, complete and accurate. That being said, however, the tax preparer is at great risk should he or she assist the taxpayer in creating information that he or she knows is a lie or that is not true, accurate and complete. The penalty for a tax preparer or any other person caught assisting a client in generating false information is much more severe than that assessed to the taxpayer *whether that person is a paid preparer or not.*

Most tax preparers and accountants solicit new clients with the express intent of taking advantage of every *legal* tax break that is available. This ilk of taxpayer is an individual that earns a reasonably good amount of money and doesn't want to give it all to the IRS. This taxpayer is ripe for any suggestion that will alleviate the tax burden and relies on the tax preparer to know the rules and which ones can be bent or broken.

When the income tax return is filed, either electronically or by paper return, there are certain areas where excessive deductions will trigger a response by the IRS computers. These are referred to as *'red flags'*. An experienced and properly trained tax preparer is aware of those red flags and will not allow his wandering client to cause the red flag to pop up. In the absence of any red flags, the probability of a tax audit is rather remote, and without an audit, a tax return with extra or false deductions will likely slip through.

Throughout the following pages, I will disclose many of the techniques that enabled me to 'assist' a goodly number of taxpayer clients in reducing their income tax liability, often to the point of zero. I have promised William that I will be totally open and hold

13

nothing back. I will even explore how and why I began to prepare income tax returns and why, how and when I found it easy to cross the line.

I would love for this recital to be completely entertaining, however, that won't be possible. I don't want my story to be boring, but, in truth, most facts are without suspense. Not as thrilling as fiction, true facts seldom sport any appealing decorations.

I will not, however, identify any of the clients with whom I have worked. Not completely. I will only use first names, and I won't promise those names will always be accurate. Nonetheless, every case is factual, every description completely accurate and each client that I am describing will know of whom I am speaking.

I also will warn you, the reader, not to use the tactics that I describe in these pages. That is, don't use them without careful research. If the reader should adopt these techniques, I suggest the reader find a good and experienced tax preparer or accountant. Or, perhaps what could be even more important, a good attorney. (Could keep you out of jail)

Hope you have as much fun reading this as we had putting it together.

~ Points to Ponder ~

~*~

"The 10,500 page Tax Code, with its endless convolutions, is an abomination unworthy of our society. Is it any surprise that some people run from under it? It undermines notion of law of, for and by the people, because even those who spend a lifetime studying can barely understand it. Certainly ordinary citizens cannot hope to figure it out."
~Treasury Secretary Paul O'Neill, March 20, 2002~

~*~

"A fine is a tax for doing something wrong. A tax is a fine for doing something right."
~Anonymous taxpayer~

~*~

"It will be of little avail to the people that the laws are made by men of their choice if the laws be so voluminous that they can not be read, or so incoherent that they cannot be understood."
~The Federalist Papers~

~*~

"The Department of Defense, in addition to paying $640.00 for a toilet seat, couldn't account for more than one trillion dollars ($1,000,000,000,000.00) of taxpayer's money...."

~San Francisco Chronicle, May

18, 2003~

Chapter 3

"Would you like to come with me to a business meeting tonight?"

Sanjiv, a brilliant young man from India, uttered those fateful words that would drastically change my life. Sanjiv had moved to Winston-Salem, North Carolina from Richmond, Virginia, where he had lived with his parents. Both his father and mother were immigrants. Without other family members nearby and with few friends, both parents were steadily employed and, in fact, each parent held down two jobs, their social life being miniscule.

Benefiting from their strong work habits, Sanjiv attended Virginia Union University, a historically black university located in Richmond. It was while at the University Sanjiv formed many of the opinions that would guide him in his future business endeavors. He formed an affinity for the lesser-privileged individuals and the thought that perhaps he could make a difference.

Sanjiv saw that the profession of preparation and electronic filing of income tax returns was a wide-open field where an aggressive person, willing to work and daring to take chances, could grow quickly. He purchased a tax preparation franchise from John Hewitt of Jackson-Hewitt Tax Service, the second largest tax preparation service company in the United States.

18

Jackson-Hewitt Tax Service sells exclusive franchises according to zip codes, one franchise per zip code. Sanjiv purchased a franchise for the zip code 27105, which covered the Northeastern part of Winston-Salem. Without another franchise near, Sanjiv actually absorbed the major part of Winston-Salem, competing with the H & R Block organization for dominance. He operated additional North Carolina offices in Concord and Kannapolis.

I met Sanjiv while I was working with Robert.

Robert and his girl friend, Carol, owned a credit repair company.

As I had been without a source of income for a while, I needed a job. I had never before been involved with credit repair. I'm sure that you know the kind of Credit Repair Company I mean.

For a few dollars, the owner of the company, Robert or his secretary-girl friend could more or less make the bad information on a credit report go away. At least, for a while.

Because of federal and state laws, Robert and Carol and any associate had to walk a fine line. To begin, a contract would be drawn up between the Credit Repair Company and the customer.

Once a contract had been signed and a deposit made, Robert or Carol would contact all of the client's debtors and, on behalf of our client, the people who were having trouble paying their bills, would offer to make small payments in return for forgiving the interest, late charges, etc. Often, these offers would only pay the debtor pennies on the dollar. Still, that was something. These offers were almost always accepted.

Under the federal and state laws, Robert could not accept the money from the client and make the payments directly to the creditors himself. It was necessary for the client to send money orders to the

19

debtors, and that the money orders be sent at the agreed time. Sometimes the client would comply with the new program, at least for a while but, more often than not, the client soon became lax. After all, most people have bad credit for a reason. They just don't pay their bills.

In different situations, Robert would send a letter to the Credit Bureau in the name of the client, protesting a delinquent account. The Credit Bureau was required to contact the merchant and solicit a response within thirty days. If no response were forthcoming, the bad credit indicator would be removed from the client's credit report. Normally, the merchant would respond and then Robert would wait 45 days and send in a second letter of protest. Again, the Credit Bureau was required to contact the merchant.

If necessary, Robert would protest the same debt several times, and eventually the merchant, or debtor, would believe that the proper answer had already been filed, and would just ignore the requirement for answering again. At that point, the record would show that the merchant did not answer the latest protest inquiry. The bad information would be erased from the record.

Robert had another interesting caper going, one in which I figured prominently. We would try to resolve business-to-business monetary judgments that one business had obtained against another.

I would research the County Court House Records of several locations across North and South Carolina, and I would obtain information regarding monetary judgments that had been filed against one business by another business. We would contact the business that owed the money and offer to have the judgment removed for less than one hundred cents on the dollar, often for only ten cents or perhaps twenty-

20

five cents on the dollar. In this manner, a ten thousand dollar judgment against a company could be settled for somewhere between one thousand and two thousand-five hundred dollars. Quite a savings for the company, and the judgment holder was often happy to receive any payment.

Of course we charged a fee, usually a percentage of what we would save the company.

This would have been an excellent career except for two things.

First, the people with a bad credit history had that bad credit history because they didn't pay anyone. Robert would accept, as our fee, a small down payment and then try to collect additional payments each week, but often the people just didn't pay. The reason they had bad credit was because they had earned it.

The second reason the job didn't pay well was that the companies with judgments against them could often settle the judgment themselves, and thereby cut us out of our fee.

The payment to me was to be a percentage of the funds collected by Robert, a commission if you will. As you may imagine, the failure of the debtor to pay resulted in low income for me, necessitating my continuing to seek additional employment elsewhere.

I had to generate income for my family and me. My reserves had been eaten up by the drug business.

~*~

No, I didn't use drugs. Never have and never will.

21

Oops, just told a lie. Actually, I will take a drink of red wine or a mixed drink on rare occasions. Guess alcohol is really a drug.

Anyway, along with my older son, I owned a home improvement company. We were doing reasonably well. Not really competing with Sears or any of the 'biggies,' however, we did excellent work and were becoming a better-known company and growing a little larger each year and we were well respected.

As we grew in size and volume, I purchased a computer, complete with bookkeeping software. Good decision, I thought.

Not!

Bad decision.

Unfortunately for me, I didn't know very much about computers. In fact, I didn't know a darn thing. But it seemed to be the coming thing, and I knew that eventually, I would have to learn to use one.

Even worse, the bookkeeping system I had learned in high school and in the military was performed using a pencil and paper. And, quite often, a very large eraser. Nothing that I had learned had anything to do with the use of a computer or its software.

Through the recommendations of an associate, a salesman employed by our firm, who is now a well-known individual prominent in the minority community, I hired a young woman to do the computer work. She had been a student at Winston Salem State and was computer-literate. Her husband was a painting contractor, and was performing subcontract work for my son and me.

Shortly before Christmas, 1991, I received a call from my bank and also received several notices by mail regarding the lack of sufficient funds to cover the checks I had issued for building materials. A member of the Forsyth County Sheriff's office visited me with a warrant for my arrest. In fact nine warrants. The charges? Issuing bad checks.

There were either nine or ten checks that had been labeled NSF, or non-sufficient funds, totaling some forty-six thousand dollars.

That just couldn't be. According to my calculations, there should have been a balance in excess of $75,000 in our bank account.

Damn. It wasn't there. But the sheriff was there and so were the bad check charges.

Later investigation efforts revealed that the young woman bookkeeper had become involved with 'crack cocaine', and had written checks to her husband and other friends that exceeded seventy thousand dollars. The checks had been written without regard to legitimate invoices and the woman, using my name, had signed all of them.

It seemed that all anyone had to do was ask her for money, and if she felt like it—or if she liked the person asking—she would draw up a check, sign my name to the check and issue it to almost anyone. All of the funds in the account were siphoned off. It was certainly no wonder that my checks bounced!

Without crying over spilled milk at this late date, the end result was that the woman, a recent mother of two beautiful twins, received probation from an understanding judge in Winston Salem, who did not order her to make restitution. Not one cent.

As for my construction company, my son and me: disaster. Total and complete disaster.

The materials suppliers who had been the recipients of worthless checks immediately shut off our credit and a large number of jobs in progress had to end. When progress on the jobs slowed, so did the payments from the homeowners with whom we were

23

working. The homeowners were funding no further monies, so the jobs were closed down.

Additionally, many of those suppliers filed criminal charges against me personally for issuing worthless checks.

Issuing and delivering a bad check is a serious crime. Only the fact that I didn't deliver the checks personally, but had sent them by mail kept me from being put into jail for any period of time. Still, a Judge in Greensboro stated that he would send me to prison if I didn't pay for one of the bad checks that had been mailed to a company in Greensboro. Guess a friend of the Judge must have owned the company.

Nonetheless, I was arrested, my fingerprints and mug shots were taken, and the charges became a part of my criminal record: a record that had not existed prior to that time. Now, I faced a severe shortage of funds for personal expenses, and had to find a job. Fast.

The job I found was with Robert and Carol. And that led to meeting Sanjiv, who was applying to work with Robert.

Had I known what the future held, I'm not exactly sure that my answer to his question would have been the same.

~It Should Make You Furious~

~*~

Did you know......

-that as of August 1, 2007, the Pentagon cannot fully account for $19 billion ($19,000,000,000.00) worth of equipment provided to Iraqi security forces? (Must be hidden with the Weapons of Mass Destruction under the sand, you think?)
~ www.newsmax.com~

-that as of December, 2005, the U.S. Government sold salvage timbers from forest fires for $8.8 million dollars? (The good news is that the cost of the sale was only $10.7 million dollars, meaning that the U.S. taxpayer only lost $2 million dollars on the sale)
~Environmental News Service~

-that of the $22.7 million dollars of U.S. taxpayer dollars funneled to the Chronic Fatigue System (CFS) during the fiscal years 1995-1998, only about $9.8 million dollars was actually spent on CFS programs activities? The remainder was spent on non-CFS activities. (Now, doesn't that just make you tired?)
~CFS/fms/mcs/lyme info~

-that the U.S. Forest Service admits that it's up a tree when it comes to collecting much

more of the $300 million dollars in logging contracts? The Forest Service has collected only 14 cents on each dollar lost to timber purchasers who defaulted on $300 million dollars.......(Guess who paid the rest? Now, doesn't that just burn your stump?)
~The Oregonian, November 20, 1993~

Chapter 4

Would you like to take a wild stab at guessing the purpose of the business meeting that I attended with Sanjiv? Have you ever heard of something called "Multi-Level Marketing?"

Well, excuse me!

I had not, at least not until that night.

Sanjiv showed up wearing a well-tailored suit (the only suit that he owned as it turned out) and had suggested that I wear a jacket and a tie. The meeting was held at the Holiday Inn on University Parkway. I won't say that I, at the tender uninformed age of 56, was the oldest one there, but there was only a few as old or older.

During the program, someone stood at a slate board and drew a bunch of circles and told me how I could become rich. All I had to do was to become a distributor of a company named Amway, and the riches would flow. Sounded good to me.

So, I did. And, of course, they didn't. Flow. Riches, that is. I was just about to learn another lesson in human frailty.

To be frank, what I saw that night did indeed open my eyes. Displayed before me was a system so simple as to be unbelievable: a system that would – or could – generate a lot of money.

Not that I'm about to convince you to become involved with Amway. In fact, I am no longer associated with the company. But that night, I saw that if I would become a distributor of Amway and either sell or buy for my own use a limited number of products that I would qualify for a small rebate. If I asked a friend to join and he or she did join and also purchased the minimum dollar amount of products, he or she would receive a rebate check, and my rebate check would increase.

How much more simple could it have been?

Still, a lot of people, some of them slightly fanatical, wanted to make more of it than it was, becoming totally immersed in the Amway movement. I thought it was quite simple, just do the minimum and have a couple of friends do the same.

Guess I'm not much of a salesman. At least, I didn't make much of a success with Amway. But there will be more about that later and you will come to see how Amway would play a large part in my efforts to help people pay fewer taxes.

~*~

I said that Sanjiv was a young man, and I do mean young. At least, he was to me. He was only about twenty-one at the time and I was in my mid-fifties. We seemed to hit it off quite well, and I was certain that, with his help, I would soon be a successful Amway distributor. And rich. Don't forget that. Rich! Me. Bill Jackson.

Meanwhile, I had need of desk space in order to process the paperwork that I was doing for Robert. Robert's office was so small there wasn't sufficient space for me to have a desk. I was hoping that if I could keep signing up additional clients fast enough, the initial payment and the few payments that Robert was able to collect would keep me afloat for a while.

Sanjiv offered to let me use space in his tax facility, which consisted of some three or four rooms, in the North Point Boulevard area of Winston Salem. It became evident that his tax business was composed almost exclusively of the electronic filing, rapid refund loan market, and after early April, he had virtually no clients until January of the following year and there was plenty of space.

I also learned that everyone called him 'Andy', which seemed to please him. I never learned why 'Andy' but assume it was to minimize the impact of a Hindu from India.

Of course, I accepted Andy's generous offer, and over the summer of 1992, I learned a lot about how income tax returns were being prepared on computers and being filed over the telephone lines, using a modem. Fascinating it was, at least to me.

And it seemed both simple and easy enough. There were a number of blank spaces on the monitor screen where you typed information. Then, you simply pushed the button, and the computer would generate the form and print out a copy. The computer would also compute the taxes due or the refund that was to be obtained.

Oh, sure. Yeah, I know.

Now it seems so commonplace. But in 1992, other than H & R Block and Jackson Hewitt, there just weren't a lot of companies doing electronic filing and rapid refund loans. And I had never used a computer, nor prepared a tax return for anyone other than my family and myself. Or, perhaps, for one of the

30

companies that I owned when I didn't have funds to pay a professional preparer or an accountant.

Still, it was easy to see that this was a market that was going to grow rapidly. And my fascination with the computerized return was nothing less than total admiration for someone's genius that could create such a system. I really wanted to be a part of that science, and the idea of preparing income taxes for others for a fee was fascinating. (Truthfully, I thought there might be a little money in it as well)

It was also about the same time that I met a black man, a close friend of Andy's from Winston Salem. Let's just call him William, as that is his first name. Yes, the same first name that you have, William. Few people knew that his name was actually William and we frequently joked about being related.

I mention his race only to let you know that we were trying to attract the minority tax-filers, most of them would qualify for the Earned Income Tax Credit and would want to file their taxes electronically in order to receive a rapid refund.

William was an accountant, well known and very active in the minority community and had been preparing taxes for clients, both businesses and individuals, for several years.

Andy had been acquainted with William for a couple of years and had agreed to provide computers and software to William that would be used in his office to prepare income tax returns for electronic filing. This would increase the number of tax returns that William could prepare. Then, Andy and William would share in the preparation and filing fees. Seemed like a good deal, at the time.

That proved to be a satisfactory, mutually rewarding arrangement, as the volume of tax returns prepared by William grew steadily over the next few

31

years. There was a strong surge during the 1993 tax season caused by reasons you will learn later, but there was bad trouble on the horizon.

~ Points to Ponder ~

~*~*

On the Internal Revenue Tax Code:
"Thousands of pages of pet rocks that have nothing to do with the national interest."
~Senator Sam Nunn, Georgia,
September 1992~

~*~

"Our tax system is complicated and unfair, and it must be eliminated."
~Richard K. Armey (R-Tex), Majority Leader of the House of Representatives
And
.....Bill Archer (R-Tex)
Chairman of the House Ways & Means Committee.
October, 2002~

~*~

"People who complain about taxes can be divided into two classes: Men and Women."
~Anonymous taxpayer~

It Should Make You Furious

Report
United States General Accounting Office
Washington, DC, 20548

Comptroller General of the United States
B-250977

June 30, 1993

To the Commissioner of the Internal Revenue
In accordance with the Chief Financial Officers
(CFO) act of 1990, the Internal Revenue Service (IRS)
prepared the accompanying Principal Financial
Statements for the fiscal year ended September 30,
1992. IRS is the largest revenue collector for the federal
government, reporting tax collections of $1.1 trillion
for fiscal year 1992........
...The results of our audit are summarized as
follows.
We *are unable* to express an opinion on the
reliability of the fiscal year 1992 Principal Financial
Statements of IRS because critical supporting
information was not available. Where supporting
information was available, we found that *such information
generally was unreliable.* As a result, internal and external
reports that were based on this information may be
unreliable.
In our opinion, internal controls were not
properly designed and implemented to effectively
safeguard assets, provide a reasonable basis for
determining material compliance with laws governing

36

the use of budget authority and other relevant laws and regulations, and assure that there were no material misstatements in the Principal Financial Statements. However, we were unable to evaluate and test all significant internal controls due to the limitations on the availability of supporting information mentioned above. (Guess you might say the IRS flunked its audit.)
~ United States General Accounting Office, June 30, 1993~

Chapter 5

A truism.

No one with whom I am acquainted enjoys paying taxes.

I don't believe any sane person would ever volunteer to pay income taxes, at least not under the current system.

We all recognize it is a necessity that we do pay taxes. Otherwise, there would be no government, and without government, no security. So taxes are a necessity. Some would say a 'necessary evil.'

And why should anyone *enjoy* the act of paying taxes? Very few of us agree with even one of the many costly programs that involves the Federal government, and not a single one of us approves of everything that the U.S. government does. Certainly, we don't approve of the way that they spend much of our money. And we don't appreciate the waste that occurs when the Federal purse strings are opened.

I'm not talking about fraud and tax cheats. Not at this point. I'm speaking of politicians and the way they spend money that is taken from us. You know what I mean, 'pork barrel spending' on their favorite projects. They trade our tax dollars for votes.

On the other hand, taking a closer look at their actions, perhaps fraud and tax cheats really are involved.

Seriously though, I'm speaking of the amount of money that the IRS takes from us to feed the Federal monster. Want a few facts?

The Tax Foundation released information about the taxpayer in the year 2006. If the average middle-income taxpayer's entire salary went to pay taxes, it would take one hundred percent of the earnings until April 26 to meet all the federal, state and local tax payments due. On average, American taxpayers now spend more time working to pay their taxes than they spend working to provide food and shelter **combined.**

Want additional facts?

'Tax Freedom Day', as it is most properly called, took place on April 26 in the year 2006. In 1930, shortly after the Great Depression started, Tax Freedom Day occurred on February 13. In 1940, the date was March 5. And it has required additional workdays each year just to pay the income tax..

And what do we get for our money? In addition to all the mismanagement that makes headline news, there is a great deal more that just doesn't get widespread attention.

One Treasury Inspector General for Tax Administration's report showed taxpayers received incorrect answers to 43 percent of tax questions that they asked an IRS agent. The investigators concluded that about 500,000 taxpayers who visited Internal Revenue Help Centers got wrong or incomplete answers.

And how could the agent not give out wrong information? The Tax Code is some 10,000 pages of the most complicated gobbledy-gook that mankind can conceive. Not even the Commissioner of the Internal Revenue is exempt from the confusion. Responding to a report of IRS employees incorrectly preparing 19 of

23 tax returns in a December 2003 survey, Commissioner Everson actually replied, "Whatever you could do to simplify the Code would really help us."

It is that complex Code, with all its inconsistencies, its loopholes and its vagueness that makes it easy for some predator, like some of my associates and me, to misuse much of the information to benefit us. Or that might benefit some client that wants to take advantage of the predator's abilities.

And there are scads of the latter.

~ Points to Ponder ~

~*~

Citing a survey showing that taxpayers annually spend more than 5 billion hours dealing with the tax system, former IRS Commissioner Fred Goldberg said, "American people have every right to demand a tax system they can live with."
~Commissioner Fred Goldberg, October 10, 1991~

~*~

"If we don't change our system of collecting taxes, it will break down....Our traditional approach cannot sustain an acceptable level of compliance."
~IRS Commissioner Shirley Peterson, January 31, 1993~

~*~

"Where deductions are based on a number of small items not susceptible to complete documentary substantiation, reasonable determinations should be made at the district examination level. Consideration will always be given to the reasonableness of the taxpayer's claimed deductions."
~IRS Policy Statement P-4-39~

It Should Make You Furious

Report
United States
General Accounting Office
Washington, DC, 20548

Comptroller General
of the United States

B-250977

June 30, 1994

To the Commissioner of the Internal Revenue

"The results of our audit of IRS' fiscal year
1993 financial statements are summarized as follows:

- We were unable to express an
opinion on the reliability of IRS's fiscal year
1993 Principal Financial Statements because (1)
critical supporting information for seized assets,
accounts payable, and collections by type of tax
was not available and (2) supporting
information for in-process revenue
transactions, tax credit balances, and funds with
Treasury was not properly analyzed and
recorded. Additionally, we noted that most
financial statement balances were unreliable due
to the errors in revenue and operating funds
transactions. As a result, internal and external
reports that were based on this information
were also unreliable. Last year, we were

44

similarly unable to express an opinion on IRS's fiscal year 1992 financial statements because complete, critical supporting information was not available and available supporting information was generally unreliable."

(No, friends, this is **not** a duplicate of an earlier report. This is a new report that for two years in a row, the IRS *couldn't be relied upon to provide accurate and correct information* to the auditors assigned by the U.S. General Accounting Office. Who is watching the "watchers?" And they actually have the nerve to talk about Anderson Accounting!)

Chapter 6

Well, now that most of the self-serving pontification is out of the way, we can get down to cases. I'll save personal disclaimers and explanations until later. In fact, there will a complete autobiography later in these pages.

As I stated earlier, most of the tax reduction antics that you will read about in these pages are based on legal provisions of the Internal Revenue Code. These are provisions that are used every tax-filing season, by virtually every professional tax preparer and by individuals who complete their own tax return.

I will be outlining and dissecting those programs and the techniques that we used for circumventing the rules and laws that apply to the programs. Some of the programs were used in a multiplicity of ways that may have benefited each client differently, so some of the information may become repetitive. I will try not to bore you with too many statistics, but I did promise to and I do want to tell the complete story. And, after all, numbers are generally boring for most people, but you may find them fascinating if you consider that we are talking about *your* dollars.

I must state that not all of the techniques were used by every one of my personal clients, although many of the techniques were used by most. A few of the techniques are ones that I spotted being used in one form or another by one or more tax preparers and filers. Although I didn't personally utilize these techniques, that doesn't make them any less interesting or less productive.

While I am setting the stage, I must give credit to certain people. At the beginning of each chapter, you will find "~ Points to Ponder ~", and other interesting tidbits. In truth, I generated only a few of the quotes, so I must admit that I stole most of the others. Guess that you can say that I'm a 'quote thief' as well as a tax cheat.

Some of the quotes are by unknown people, and others are identified when I was able to determine the source. A few of the quotes were discovered in Jeff A. Schnepper's 'HOW TO PAY ZERO TAXES', a publication that gives the tax-filer a lot of good information as well as the proper, and legal, way to use that information to their benefit.

Other quotes were taken from various sources, including the IRS 'Humorous Site', although the idea of humor and the IRS is an oxymoron. Nevertheless, there were a mixture of deadly serious articles and humorous quotations found, and I have tried to use them as a 'short commercial break' between chapters.

The commercial break is for me because you would not believe the turmoil that occurs in a man's mind when he is trying to relate how he dared to challenge the Internal Revenue Service.

Unfortunately, unlike Don Quixote's, the IRS windmill really is a dragon!

And my steed wasn't a fast Arab, but a broken down old plug.

~ Points to Ponder ~

~*~

Rep. Jim Saxton (R-NJ) reported in the United States House of Representatives on May 7, 2005, that taxpayers with income greater than $200,000 will see their share of the income tax burden increase from 44.8 percent to 45.5 percent, and will receive an average 10.8 percent CUT in income taxes. Taxpayers with income between $30,000 and $40,000 will see a tax reduction of 19.3 percent, reducing their share of taxes from 2.1 percent to 1.9 percent. (Huh? Run that one by me just one more time.)

~*~

"Our current tax system is an abomination."
~U.S. Treasury Secretary Paul O'Neill, May 17, 2001~

~*~

"I don't think you can take the tax system seriously anymore."
~Christopher S. Rizek, formerly Associate Tax Legislative Counsel~

~*~

"Only feeble minds are paralyzed by facts."
~Arthur C. Clark, Science
Fiction writer~

Chapter 7

As a rule, the normal period of income tax return filing runs from early January through mid-April. Of course there are often a few stragglers, but for the most part the tax returns are filed before the tax-filing deadline in mid-April.

The electronic filing season is somewhat different. Most of the patrons of an electronic filing firm are of the lower income bracket, seeking a rapid refund. In fact, many of these clients depend upon that refund to pay rent or to by food. Sometimes, to buy drugs.

The idea of receiving a tax refund is exciting to all of us, even the more affluent. The concept of a 'tax refund' is not difficult to appreciate; it's something like receiving money from a distant relative. The difference is that, in most cases, the refund that you receive is actually your own money, withheld from your wages and used by the U.S. government for a year without paying interest and without so much as a 'thank-you'.

That's correct. The basic reason most people qualify for a tax refund is that the employer withheld an excessive amount, and the United States government has had the use of that money for a year or so, interest free. In brief, the government kept your money, used it, and now is refunding some of it, and without paying you one thin dime of interest.

Just think. What if you could borrow money from a bank, or buy a house or a car without paying interest. Perhaps you would like to use your credit card without paying interest. No, you can't do it. But, the government can, and the government does.

There are only a few exceptions, but there is one particular program that actually refunds money to certain individuals whether or not there has been withholding. That program is known as the Earned Income Tax Credit.

This is a provision in the Internal Revenue Service Code that is designed to help the lower-income people who have dependent children. That procedure, known as the Earned Income Tax Credit, is one area where tax cheats find it easy to operate. And it is there they find the most willing and least knowledgeable tax filer.

The United States Federal Earned Income Tax Credit (EITC) is a refundable tax credit that reduces or eliminates the taxes that low-income people pay, such as payroll taxes, and also frequently operates as a wage subsidy for low-income workers. Enacted in 1975, the then very small EITC was expanded in 1986, 1990, 1993 and 2001 with each major tax bill, regardless of whether the tax bill in general raised taxes (1990), lowered taxes (2001), or eliminated other deductions and credits (1986). The EITC is one of the most promoted anti-poverty tools in the United States and enjoys broad bipartisan support in all branches of the federal government.

The EITC is also the area were fraud and fraudulent tax returns are most often detected. Because the EITC is basically free money, there are many different methods that are used by tax preparers and tax-filers alike, trying to get part of the pie.

Because most of the EITC is funded to the lower-income wage earners, the appeal of filing quickly by electronic means and obtaining a fast refund by means of a refund anticipation loan, proves to be an irresistible lure to many lower-income tax-filers. Once a form W-2 is received, there would be a mad rush to the nearest electronic tax-filer to obtain the money as quickly as possible.

The electronic tax filing combined with the EITC bonus results in many of the lower income tax-filers having their returns prepared and filed as early as possible, because often the return rebate may be of some significant amount.

In the 1992 tax season, with the income tax returns being filed between January 1993 and April 1993, an income tax-filer with an income of less than $22,370.00 would qualify for the earned income tax credit, providing the tax-filer had a child. With one child and with an income between $7,500.00 and $11,850.00, the tax-filer would receive the maximum earned income tax credit payment for each child, up to a limit of two children. If the tax-filer was at that income level and had one child the tax credit payment was $1,324.00. For the same tax-filer with two children the tax credit payment was $1,384.00. The credit was a payment by the U.S. Government and was in addition to any other amount of refund that might be due.

By the tax year 2005, the numbers had increased drastically, growing more each year. For a tax-filer in the year 2005 (filing between January and April, 2006), the maximum income for a person to obtain an earned income tax credit had grown to $35,263.00. Or, $37,263 provided that the tax-filer was married and filing a joint return. The amount of the earned income tax credit payment became $2,662.00 for one child and $4,400.00 for two children.

In order to obtain the earned income tax credit, the tax-filer must have a qualifying dependent. In 1992, that designation was son, daughter or grandchild.

During recent years, that designation has grown to include "Child", "Nephew" and "Niece".

The information that the tax-filer had to provide was the name, date of birth, relationship and social security number of the dependent claimed.

One of the quirks of electronic filing of income tax returns, is that the first person to file a child as a qualifying child receives the earned income tax credit. Once one taxpayer has claimed a child, the IRS computer will not allow another taxpayer to claim the same child.

While preparing and filing income tax returns in 1992, it was obvious that there was very little crosschecking by the Internal Revenue Service, and the only thing a tax-filer had to possess in order to claim a child as a qualifying dependent was the date of birth and the social security number.

There were many tax-filers who had no dependent in 1991 and, miraculously, in 1992 had a dependent as old as 16 years of age.

During that tax-filing season, many income tax filing firms, including the one that I was working with, explored and capitalized on the market, a market that was destined to grow at a rapid pace.

The firm that could prepare a tax return and obtain a rapid refund loan for the tax-filer in the shortest period of time would get the lion's share of the market.

Sanjiv and I were able to perform that service in less than twelve hours.

~ Points to Ponder ~

~*~

"The words of such an act as the Income Tax...merely dance before my eyes in a meaningless procession; cross-reference, exception upon exception—couched in abstract terms that offer no handle to seize hold of—leave in my mind only a confused sense of some vitally important, but successfully concealed, purport, which it is my duty to extract, but which is within my power, if at all, only after the most inordinate expenditure of time. I know that these monsters are the result of fabulous industry and ingenuity, plugging up this hole and casting out the net, against all invasion; yet at times I cannot help recalling a saying of William James about certain passages of Hegel: that they were, no doubt, written with a passion of rationality; but that one cannot help wondering whether to the reader they have any significance save that the words are strung together with syntactical correctness..."
~Judge Learned Hand, the Thomas Walter Swan,   57 Yale Law Journal 167, 169 (1947)~

~*~

"Take it off. Take it all off."
.....Gypsy Rose Lee, Entertainer

It Should Make You Furious

Doing Well by Doing Good.

The Baltimore Public Housing Authority's (PHA) operations are funded largely by the U.S. Department of Housing and Urban Development (HUD)—$52 million in operating subsidies for FY 1994—and the PHA has a waiting list of 25,000 poor families in line for housing assistance. Yet the Baltimore authority was found to have improperly used the public's—(read "taxpayer's") money by buying eight new Chevy Blazers as take-home cars for its top managers, hiring a high-bid security firm that employed 29 convicted felons, and spending more than $25 million of building repair funds on no-bid contracts to contractors, including some who were friends and relatives of Authority employees.

HUD asked that $725,000 be returned because of inflated costs or work never completed. Despite this record of mismanagement, HUD just awarded the same housing authority $115 million to construct 338 new apartment units for the poor as part of a court-imposed desegregation settlement.

Who's in Charge: Kevin E. Marchman, HUD's Assistant Secretary-Designated for Public and Indian Housing, (202) 708-0950.

See Audit Report, Office of the Inspector General: U.S. Department of Housing and Urban Development, No. 94-PH-201-1016. September 23, 1994.

(Guess the felons were to take the blame.)

Chapter 8

And now, it begins.

A great way to bribe people is to give them money.

The Split Family Caper

The ever-increasing amount of the Earned Income Tax Credit refund and the inability of the Internal Revenue Service to be able to constantly monitor or check all of the tax returns being filed made it a simple matter for the tax-filer to cheat. Especially if he or she was working with a tax preparer that believed that it wasn't part of the responsibility of the tax preparer to verify all of the information provided by the tax-filer.

The IRS and the U.S. government had made it virtually impossible for the tax preparer to verify the information in any case, as there were laws enacted that would not allow the tax preparer to access the social security records and other data bases maintained by the government. The tax preparer was literally forced to accept at face value any information provided by the tax-filer. In fact, most tax preparers preferred to remain behind the screen, so as to avoid liability in the event of a fraudulent tax return.

~*~

The Internal Revenue Code allows for certain filing status. If a person is single, than he or she files the tax return as 'single'. If the person is married, then the choice is either: 'married, filing separately' or 'married, filing jointly'. If a person is considered unmarried, but has a child living in the same household, then the person may qualify as 'head of house'. Each filing status has some benefits and some inconveniences.

To qualify for the Earned Income Tax Credit, it was necessary to have a qualifying child, and as earlier mentioned, at the time of which I am writing, that child had to be a direct bloodline descendent, i.e. a son, daughter, grandson or granddaughter.

Many of the tax-filers and all of the tax preparers knew the rules. If a couple were married, they were supposed to file their income tax return under one of the filing status situations that existed, either married filing joint or married filing separately. Often, even regularly, that rule was circumvented, especially when there was more than one child.

The husband would file his income tax returns listing an address. He would claim the 'head of household' status. If there were two children, he would use one as a dependent and as a qualifying child. In this manner, he would receive up to eighteen hundred dollars extra in his refund.

The wife would then file her income tax return listing a different address, most often the address of a relative or a post office box. She would also claim the 'head of household' status and would use at least one child to qualify for the Earned Income Tax Credit. Thus, she would receive the extra one thousand eight hundred dollars in turn.

Filing as two separate 'head of household' individuals, the standard deductions for each would add up to substantially more than if the two should file in their correct status of either 'married filing jointly' or 'married filing separately.' In addition, the two Earned Income Tax Credits would amount to three thousand six hundred dollars, which would be roughly twice as much as they would have received had the returns been accurately prepared.

In fact, had the two filed as 'married filing jointly', it is likely that their joint income may have completely disqualified them from receiving the tax credit. And, of course, filing as 'married filing separately', both would have been disqualified from receiving Earned Income Tax Credits.

When the tax returns were prepared in this manner, should there have been a third child, the child would have been added to the tax return of the person who would benefit the most for the added child. Earned Income Tax Credits could increase from three thousand six hundred dollars for one child to five thousand four hundred dollars for two children.

In a like manner, sometimes a single parent with two or more children would 'loan' a child or two to a neighbor, a boy friend (or a girl friend), or to another individual.

Sometimes the tax preparer may well have been aware of what was happening, but preferred to bury his or her head in the sand and pretend that everything was proper. The bonus was that the tax preparer would be paid for preparing two income tax returns instead of one, even if the tax preparer did not participate in the excess tax credit dollars that the two tax-filers received (which was not always the case).

~ Points to Ponder ~

~*~

"Our income tax system is overly complex. It distorts investment decisions and encourages people to put money into schemes to reduce their tax bills instead of into enterprises that creates jobs and helps our economy grow.:
~Bill Bradley, New Jersey Senator (1984)~

~*~

"About 948,000 taxpayers in the past year failed to itemize their deductions, even though they qualified to do so, resulting in a $473 million dollar overpayment in taxes.
~General Accounting Office, April 11, 2002~

~*~

As a citizen, you have an obligation to the country's tax system, but you also have an obligation to yourself to know your rights under the law and possible tax deductions. And to claim every one of them.
~Donald Alexander, former commissioner of the IRS under three presidents~

It Should Make You Furious

........They All Threatened to Leave.

According to the U.S. General Accounting Office and the U.S. Office of Personnel Management, 95 percent of the bonuses recently granted by the managers of the U.S. Export-Import Bank to their employees were "improper and excessive" and cost the taxpayer as much as $1 million in overpayments.

According to the GAO, 1995 bonuses were granted to 200 of the Bank's 448 employees, but only 10 of the 200 employees were actually eligible to receive the money. Ex-Im's bonus abuse was uncovered a year earlier when a GAO audit revealed that just five government agencies accounted for 94 percent of these special retention bonuses. Although the Ex-Im Bank had the smallest work force of the five agencies reviewed, it accounted for 25 percent of all bonuses government-wide, and the GAO auditors noted that many of these awards "did not appear to comply with the statutory requirement."

Whereas the Department of Defense granted such bonuses to only 0.03 percent of its work force in 1994, 21 percent of Ex-Im employees received such bonuses that year, and nearly 45 percent received them in 1995. Although the Office of Personnel Management stripped the acting head of the Ex-IM Bank of his authority to grant bonuses, his April 1996 recess appointment to the top Bank post by President Clinton was accompanied by the reinstatement of bonus-granting authority.

And although Ex- Im. Bank officials have argued that they are merely continuing Bush Administration practices; the GAO audit indicates that the Ex-Im Bank granted no such bonuses during those years.

Who's in Charge: Martin Kamarck, President and Chairman-Designate of the Export-Import Bank, (202) 565-3500.

(And 'they' thought that all Bill did was to smoke cigars and sell a few pardons.)

Chapter 9

The 'Genie-in-a-Bottle' Dependent Caper

By the time the following 1993 tax filing season started, I had come to appreciate the electronic filing process and had become somewhat adept using the programs and the software. Completing income tax returns required little or no knowledge about the legality of the entries, only the knowledge that certain information had to be entered into certain blank spaces in order to generate a completed tax return. And, depending on the information entered into each blank space, different results would appear. Juggling those entries or adjusting the numbers could produce the results that one wanted.

It was also at this point that the Internal Revenue decided to make it convenient for the tax-filer and the preparer to falsify tax returns. A modification of the social security number requirement for electronic filing took place. And business boomed.

For the 1992 income tax year and prior to that, the actual social security number had to be entered into the proper blank space on the tax form. If a child was born too late in 1991 to obtain a social security number before the return was prepared in early 1992, then the return could not be filed electronically, unless the child was omitted. This meant that the tax-filer would have to wait several weeks for their refund, thus reducing the desirability of paying extra for electronic filing.

The Internal Revenue Service didn't want to discourage electronic filing. Oh, no. Not in the slightest.

After all, we were doing most of their work for them if we prepared the return and filed it electronically. If all tax returns were prepared and filed electronically, the need for data entry people at the income tax centers would be greatly reduced, allowing more funds to give the supervisors a pay increase or to spend in other foolish ways. (No, they were not about to give you a tax rebate. Are you kidding?)

The hierarchy of the IRS decided to permit tax-filers to claim dependents born late in the year, and modified their requirements to allow the word "APPLIED" to be substituted for the social security, providing that the birth date was later than September 30 of the tax year.

Oops. The IRS really shouldn't have done that.

That really opened the floodgates.

Prior to 1993, William (the other "William", guess I will have to call him William P.) had his own self-benefit program in operation. The ruse that William P. would perform in order to increase the refund of his clients was to 'share dependents'. In the lower-income minority market that William P. serviced, there were frequently families that had more dependents than they actually needed to claim in order to obtain the maximum refund.

Once the maximum refund amount was achieved, the surplus dependents would be bartered to another family or a tax-filer that didn't have dependents. The going price in 1992 was roughly six hundred dollars per child. As the tax-filer would gain more than thirteen hundred dollars in additional refunds, the tax-filer willingly agreed to pay six hundred dollars and keep more than seven hundred dollars that the tax-filer would not have received without the dependent. William P. was one of the first 'child-brokers' in the industry, wheeling and dealing dependents as if they were used cars. (Don't believe that William P. did it all for charity. He certainly got his cut.)

William P. wasn't the only one plying his trade. It's my understanding that classes were often held in church meeting rooms and basements to educate the tax filing community about the procedures involved in maximizing the tax refund, including trading children and other dependents.

William P. would prepare income tax returns for both tax-filers. The filer obtaining the new dependent would receive at least a $1,300.00 additional refund because of the earned income tax credit payment. Of that $1,300.00 he or she or they would pay William P. $600.00 or $700.00. In turn, William P. would pay the tax-filer giving up the dependent between $200.00 and $400.00, pocketing the rest. Everyone was happy, as everyone benefited. It was only later that trouble began to arise as it developed that William P. was just a little too greedy.

In the tax year 1993, the acceptance of the word 'APPLIED' in lieu of an actual social security number had a disastrous result for the Internal Revenue Service. The number of dependents being born between October 1, 1992 and December 31, 1992 went through the roof. Virtually every tax-filer had at least two children, often with both children being born in late 1992.

It must have been a modern day miracle that the hospitals were able to manage the fantastic number of new births that occurred during those 90 days. Tax-

68

filers as young as eighteen, and without the blessings of matrimony, became instant parents of twins, while tax-filers with one legitimate child often found themselves with another 'unexpected' child.

Of course, these 'miracle' children increased the refund that the tax-filer received, and, to my knowledge, there was not a single objection by any of the tax-filers. At Andy's offices, all of the preparers were aware of the potential, but no one was allowed to charge additional fees even if a magical dependent appeared. Andy had attended Virginia Union University and because of the darkness of his skin, had felt at home with the minority students. It was his opinion that he was only helping the poor tax-filers get money that they deserved anyway.

While it is an absolute that we didn't charge additional fees at these offices (except possibly William P.), it is also true that we filed a total of six thousand three hundred tax returns that year, which was an increase of almost fifty percent And Andy was most pleased. Me? I was just pooped.

At the main office in Winston-Salem, we were open twenty-four hours a day, and it was taking its toll on all of us.

My oldest son had come aboard and was helping prepare the tax returns. At first, he knew as little as I had known when I began, but quickly became a competent preparer. Then, he became inured in the process, as did most of the other tax preparers. In his words, "You just won't believe the sh*t that we did for—and with— our clients. And for no monetary reward."

Thank Heavens for Amway Vitamins and for Taco Bell Burritos (not that the burritos were especially good, but Taco Bell was near-by and was open until two am). And I'm certain that the vitamins that we all ordered from the Amway Company enabled us to survive.

We would often work twenty-four hours or longer without sleep; stop and catch a few hours of sleep in one of the back rooms and then go back to work. It was hectic, but was also a lot of fun. But trouble was brewing; trouble generated by William P.

It wasn't until somewhat later that we discovered another ruse that had been used by William P. He would often prepare a tax return for an individual and give that individual a copy of that return showing a modest tax refund. William P. would then modify the return by adding a dependent that would increase the amount of refund by more than $1,300.00. He would do this without the knowledge of the tax-filer. He would file the income tax return using a post office box that he had rented as the return mail address. Checks mailed to those tax-filers arrived at his post office box from not only the Federal income tax authorities but also state income tax refund checks from the State Department of Revenue. William P. would cash those checks, and then pay the tax-filer the amount of refund he or she was expecting, but which was somewhat less than the original amount of the check. William P. would keep the balance. It was this practice, and his continued greed, that would get him, and us, into trouble at a later date.

~ Points to Ponder ~

~*~

"As to the astuteness of taxpayers in ordering their affairs so as to minimize taxes, it has been said that the very meaning of a line in the law is that you intentionally may go as close to it as you can if you do not pass it."

> ~Superior Oil Co v Mississippi, 280 U.S. 390, 395-96~

~*~

"This is so because nobody owes any public duty to pay more than the law demands; taxations are enforced extractions, not voluntary contributions."

> ~J. Frankfurter, Atlantic Coast Line v Phillips, 322 U.S. 168   172-73 (1947)~

~*~

"Democracy must be something more than two wolves and a sheep voting on what to have for dinner."

> .....Robert A. Heinlein

It Should Make You Furious

GAO REPORTS ON THE IRS
AUGUST 4, 1995

REPORT NUM: AIMD-95-141

TITLE: Financial Audit: Examination of IRS'
Fiscal Year 1994

Financial Statements
DATE: 08/04/95
SUBJECT: Financial statement audits

B-259455

To the Commissioner of Internal Revenue
In accordance with the Chief Financial Officers
(CFO) Act of 1990, the Internal Revenue Service (IRS)
prepared the accompanying Principal Financial
Statements for the fiscal years ended September 30,
1994 and 1993. We were unable to express an opinion
on the reliability of these statements for the following
five primary reasons.

One, the amount of total revenue of $1.3
trillion reported in the financial statements could not be
verified or reconciled to accounting records maintained
for individual taxpayers in the aggregate.

Two, amounts reported for various types of
taxes collected, for example, social security, income,
and excise taxes, could also not be substantiated.

Three, we could not determine from our
testing of IRS' gross and net accounts receivable

74

estimates of over $69 billion and $35 billion, respectively, which include delinquent taxes, whether those estimates were reliable.

Four, IRS continued to be unable to reconcile its Fund Balance with Treasury accounts.

Five, we could not substantiate a significant portion of IRS' $2.1 billion in non-payroll expenses included in its total operating expenses of $7.2 billion, primarily because of lack of documentation. However, we could verify that IRS properly accounted for and reported its $5.1 billion of payroll expenses.

Also, continuing material weaknesses in internal controls in fiscal year 1994 resulted in ineffective controls for safeguarding assets; providing a reasonable basis for determining material compliance with laws governing the use of budget authority and other relevant laws and regulations; and assuring that there were no material misstatements in its Principal Financial Statements, including the Overview to the Financial Statements as well as supplemental information.

In addition to these problems, as discussed in subsequent sections of this report, we also identified other unsubstantiated and/or misstated amounts, such as $6.5 billion in contingent liabilities that were unsubstantiated. The differences we identified for specific reported amounts in IRS' financial statements could in fact be larger or smaller than the tens of billions of dollars discussed in this report. IRS did not know, and we could not determine, the reasons for most of the differences. Therefore, we could not adequately estimate appropriate adjustments to make the statements more reliable.

(Wake up out there! These people are in charge of our nation's finances)

Chapter 10

The IRS Strikes Back

While the golden goose wasn't exactly killed in the tax year 1994, it was certainly badly maimed.

The number one attraction of electronic filing was the Refund Anticipation Loan program. That is the means by which an electronic filer obtains early access to the tax refund. A bank, perhaps Bank One or Citi Bank, participates by making a loan to the tax-filer, known as an RAL, or Refund Anticipation Loan.

The method in use was that when the income tax return was prepared and electronically filed through the tax preparation software provider, the return was filed simultaneously with the Internal Revenue Service and the Refund Anticipation Loan bank. The bank determined the credit worthiness of the tax-filer, while the IRS determined if there was a lien on the tax-filer or any derogatory information that would cause the refund to be denied. If there weren't a problem, the IRS would send an indicator to the bank that the refund would likely be made. The bank would then make a loan to the tax-filer, at a huge interest rate of course, and would authorize the tax preparer to issue a refund anticipation loan check. The bank fees and the tax preparation fees would be deducted before the check was written.

As the tax-filer received an early refund, the tax preparer received his fees and the bank received their interest, everyone was happy. Except for the IRS. And, of course, the IRS had the hammer. A mighty big hammer. And they used it.

Perhaps it was because the IRS didn't participate in the proceeds, or perhaps the authorities had determined there had been copious fraud during the prior year, but in January 1995, the IRS suddenly changed its procedures and refused to send the indication signal to the banks.

Banks, being banks, did what banks always do. They quit making loans. The banks suddenly pulled in their horns. Absent the indicator, the bank would have to make a decision on its own whether or not to make the loan. And the response was to stop the loans. Virtually a complete, sudden, unexpected halt, and there was no warning to the public and certainly not to the tax preparer.

Did you read about the tax preparer that was assaulted and badly beaten in a tax preparation office in Atlanta, Georgia? Or the tax preparer that was shot in St. Louis, Missouri? Or the many other cases where offices were ransacked by irate tax-filers who had been relying on the refund anticipation loans?

Even in Winston Salem, we had to confront many angry tax-filers. Threats and attempted violence was frequent. We didn't close our doors, but were severely tempted.

I stand 6'3" and weigh about 220 pounds (at that time, anyway). Not exactly a lightweight, and not badly out of condition. (Things, and I, have certainly changed.) But I was scared sh......er, frightened by the

77

fiery riled and rabid tax-filers, especially the female minority single parents who were certain that it was the tax preparer's fault and that we should be punished. Razors and knives were displayed and even guns were brandished to threaten. On several occasions, only the fact that we prepared also income tax returns for many of the Winston-Salem police (yes, they paid), and one of the policemen was usually in attendance, kept us from being treated worse than we were.

Finally, the situation calmed down a little, as the banks, at the request of the IRS, began to make partial loans that were much smaller than the amount that the tax-filer was anticipating. That action alleviated the situation to a degree. At least we were able to complete the season in one piece. But the number of returns prepared dropped drastically from more than six thousand to less than three thousand. We suffered, not only for that year, but also for following years.

Another blow that fell was that the IRS insisted that every dependent must have a proper social security number if the tax return was to be filed electronically. Hospitals began obtaining those numbers for newborn babies at birth, so the use of the word 'applied' was no longer permissible.

Oh well. Back to the good old tax manipulation manual. And the search was on for another golden goose. And it suddenly appeared, brought forth by William P. and what he had been doing in earlier years.

~ Points to Ponder ~

~*~

"If we don't do something to simplify the tax system, we're going to end up with a national police force of internal revenue agents."
~Leon Panetta~

~*~

"A tax expert is someone who learns more and more about less and less until he or she knows absolutely everything about absolutely nothing."
~Unknown Sage~

~*~

"Day in and day out, your tax accountant can make or lose you more money than any single person in your life, with the possible exceptions of your kids."
~Harvey Mackay~

It Should Make Your Furious

Did you know.....

• During the past five years, the United States foreign operations appropriations for the **People's Republic of China** has more than doubled, from $10 million in FY 2002 to $23 million in FY 2006?

• American consumers (read "taxpayers") pay a heavy price to subsidize the sugar barons, of whom some of the richest are foreign citizens. The brothers Alfonso Jr. (Alfie) and Jose (Pepe) Fanjul, immigrants from Cuba but citizens of Spain, possess a fortune estimated at over $500 million. This fortune includes several Florida sugar mills, 170,000 acres of cane in south Florida, and another 240,000 acres of land in the Dominican Republic. As "domestic" growers, they are entitled to the sugar import protection enforced by the U.S. Department of Agriculture, which adds about 8 cents per pound to what the American consumer pays for sugar and about $65 million to the annual income of the Fanjuls. As if this were not enough government help, the Fanjuls' other business interests have benefited from federal, state, and local affirmative action programs that provide minority set-asides for qualified firms. For

example, the Fanjuls' investment firm, FAIC
Securities, enjoys the right to market the debt
of Florida municipalities and such government-
sponsored enterprises as the Federal National
Mortgage Association and the Federal Home
Loan Banks.

Who's in Charge: Daniel Glickman,
Secretary of Agriculture, (202) 720-363 1.
~Heritage Foundation
Research/Economy/FYI105~

(Don't you just love to see your tax dollars at
work benefiting the poor and downtrodden? And the
American taxpayer is supporting Communist China?
Sure, let's build up our future enemy.)

Chapter 11

The 'Shared Dependent' Caper

Actually, I fibbed. There really isn't a 'tax manipulation instruction manual'. Nor is there a school where one can learn the tricks that an IRS cheat might practice. One learns by observing other tax preparers, listening when one is speaking and by trial and error.

Earlier, I stated that the Earned Income Tax Credit was beneficial to families with certain income levels and with one or two children. If the tax-filer's income was low enough to qualify for the EITC, it wasn't likely that there would be any tax liability, and that the tax-filer would receive the maximum refund for one or two children.

In many of the lower-income workers' families, there are often more than two children. One instance I remember in particular involved eleven children, all under the age of eighteen, in just one family. Amazing, considering that the total reportable income to the family was less than fifteen thousand dollars for the entire year. Using two children on the family tax return would generate the maximum refund and the remaining nine children would not add to the refund. The remaining children were 'leased' to the tax preparer or another tax-filer.

Nine children multiplied by five hundred dollars or by seven hundred dollars amounts to a sum between four thousand five hundred dollars and six thousand and three hundred dollars. That was almost one-half as much as the tax-filer had earned for the entire year.

Do you think the tax-filer was reluctant to enroll in the 'Shared Dependents' operation?

Even in other cases where there happened to be only one or two unneeded dependents, an additional five hundred to two thousand dollars was very attractive. Especially appealing to the newer tax-filers among the Hispanic market, who were earning as much for one shared dependent as the family would earn working for three months in their home country. Explanations were not always needed; only the mention of the sum of money and the tax-filer would provide dates of birth, social security numbers and copies of the birth certificate, when requested.

If the tax-filer had used one of our offices to prepare his income tax for the prior year, that information would already be in our computers, and easily accessible to the tax preparer. It really wasn't necessary to ask permission, or to explain what was taking place, as the mere hint of additional monies was generally sufficient.

The same procedure was available in other low-income workers' markets, provided that the worker had more than two dependents.

Sharing of dependent occurred mostly with minorities, including Hispanics and African-Americans, as they constituted the majority of the low-income clients. While it wasn't really necessary to get too deep into details with most of the Hispanics, it was even less a need to explain the program to the single mother of the African-American community. It may or may not have been true but William P. assured me that during the early and mid-1990's, seminars were being held in the basement of churches and community buildings to teach people how to use the Earned Income Tax Credit program to their own benefit.

At that particular time, the Internal Revenue Service computers were running behind the electronic filing program, and it was relatively simple for a person not to have a dependent during one year and then have two the next year. Provided, of course, that the needed information – date of birth, name and social security number was correct.

During more recent years, there has been a lot of attention paid to this area, and if a tax-filer doesn't have a dependent this year and then claims a dependent the subsequent year, the IRS computers will generate a 'red flag', often resulting in the tax return being delayed, pending verification of the change.

Even so, the Shared Dependents manipulations are alive and well. And in use in virtually every area of the United States.

~ Points to Ponder ~

~*~

"Our party has been accused of fooling the public by calling tax increases 'revenue enhancement'. Not so! No one was fooled."
~J. Danforth Quayle, V.P. 1989-1993~

~*~

"If Patrick Henry thought that taxation without representation was bad, he should see how bad it is with representation."
~Old Farmer's Almanac~

~*~

"There's nothing more dangerous than the U.S. Congress with an idea."
~E. Patrick McGuire of the Conference Board, opening a Conference Examining Tax Incentives~

~*~

"The alternative minimum tax is a 'perfect example' of a lack of common sense in the tax code..."
~Nina Olson, National Taxpayer Advocate~

It Should Make You Furious

Did You Know......

- that government support is about 300 percent greater than private support with the U.S. Government being the largest grantor in the world?
- that the U.S. government has over 1,368 federal programs that provide assistance to the American public?
- buried in the Department of the Treasury's '2003 Financial Report of the United States Government' is a short section titled "Unreconciled Transactions Affecting Change in Net Position," which explains that these unreconciled transactions total $24.5 billion in 2003. The unreconciled transactions are funds for which auditors cannot account. The government knows that $25 billion was spent by someone, somewhere, on something, but auditors do not know *who* spent it, *where* it was spent, or on *what* it was spent?"
- a recent audit revealed that between 1997 and 2003, the Defense Department purchased and then left unused approximately 270,000 commercial airline tickets at a total cost of $100 million. Even worse, the Pentagon never bothered to get refunds for these *fully refundable* tickets. Auditors

90

also found 27,000 transactions between 2001 and 2002 in which the Pentagon paid twice for the same ticket. The department would purchase the ticket directly and then inexplicably reimburse the employee for the cost of the ticket. In one case, an employee who allegedly made seven false claims for airline tickets professed not to have noticed that $9,700 was deposited into his/her account. These additional transactions cost taxpayers $8 million.

~Source: Heritage Organization Research/Budget/bg1840.cfm~

(After spending $640 each for toilet seats, guess this seemed to be too good a bargain to pass up.)

Chapter 12

The Illegal Immigrant Caper

The title, 'Illegal Immigrant', may be slightly misleading. In 1995, there was no great uproar about whether or not a person was an immigrant, or if he or she were legal or illegal. The illegal immigrant was not the political football that it seems to be today. Everyone was aware of the facts, but everyone turned his or her back, ignoring the situation and paying scant attention to the immigrant's status. In fact, there was no way that a tax preparer could obtain the information needed to make that determination.

Nonetheless, there were many occasions when the Internal Revenue Service computer would not accept the social security number of the tax-filer.

Perhaps a word of explanation is in order. When a tax return is prepared, all blank spaces must be filled in, including the social security numbers. The social security numbers submitted must match the records maintained by the Social Security Department. If those numbers do not match, the return is rejected and can't be filed electronically. The return must then be submitted by mail, if it is filed at all.

If the immigrant is not in the United States legally, he or she can't legally obtain a valid social security number. However, in order to obtain employment, the immigrant – the person – must have a social security number.

The person obtains that number in one of two ways. The person either borrows a social security number from someone or buys one from a source. Often the number is borrowed from a relative or a friend, who is not working, and thus the number would be a valid number and the IRS computers would then accept the return.

It is only in recent years that the name, social security number and date of birth must all match for the return to be accepted electronically, but in the mid-1990's, there was no such crosscheck. Anyone could file using any social security number, providing that the number had actually been issued to someone—either the tax-filer or someone else—by the Social Security Department. Therefore the return, prepared using a valid social security number—regardless to whom it belonged—would be accepted by the Internal Revenue Service computer, processed and the refund would be made.

The second procedure, buying a social security number, often resulted in a completely false social security number. In as much as the number was bogus, the IRS computers could not accept the return. Once the return was rejected, the tax-filer would have to send the return by mail. In most cases, the refund would be granted and a check would be mailed to the immigrant.

To the tax preparer, it was relatively simple. If the return was transmitted electronically and accepted by the Internal Revenue Service, the preparer's fees would be deducted from the refund by the bank making the Refund Anticipation Loan. If the return had to be sent by mail, the tax preparer collected the fees in advance from the tax-filer.

The person, illegal or legal, knew that failure to file income tax returns was a severe crime, even worse than simply being an illegal immigrant. Further, when or if the immigrant applied for either legal status or citizenship, one of the requirements was a copy of the income tax returns for the years that the immigrant had been in the United States. For this reason, the immigrant, even if he or she were not in the United States legally, were eager to file a tax return.

One boon to the 'Shared Dependent Market' was the size of the average immigrant family. Most of the immigrants were Hispanic and often had more than two children. As the Earned Income Tax Credit only applied to two children, the remaining children were 'surplus' and the immigrant, sometimes without his or her knowledge, shared their children with others who had no children.

Another pleasant surprise was that the children of the illegal immigrant were often possessors of legitimate social security numbers. If a child is born in the United States (even today), that child is an American citizen and is entitled to a social security number. Most immigrants are aware of this and will enter the United States illegally or on a tourist visa for the express purpose of giving birth to a child in the United States. As the child is a US citizen with a valid social security number, the child can become eligible for social security benefits at the normal retirement age.

In the interim, as the income tax return could not be filed electronically, the children of the illegal immigrant would be bartered to a tax-filer who needed a dependent or two. Normally it was accomplished with the permission of the immigrant, but not always. It is a fact that the IRS computers, at that time, did not crosscheck dependents on electronic filings with dependents on paper returns.

94

I'm sure you would have found it remarkable as to how many Anglo-Saxon or African-American tax-filers suddenly had children of Hispanic origin. And I'll bet that you thought that the different races just couldn't get along.

It is also surprising to learn how many tax preparers were completely unknowledgeable and unaware that some tax filers were actually sharing their dependents. And were sharing their refunds, as well. At least, the preparers pretended to be unaware. Naturally. You know, like the ostrich. Would you believe 'head in the sand'?

These tactics benefited many of the lower-income and lower-middle income tax brackets, but did not benefit them all.

However, there were other methods.

~ Points to Ponder ~

~*~

"Where there's a single thief, it's robbery.
Where there are a thousand thieves, it's taxation."
~Vanya Cohen~

~*~

"To tax and to please, nor more than to love
and to be wise, is not given to men."
~Edmund Burke, 18th Century Irish political
philosopher and British statesman~

~*~

"Like mothers, taxes are often misunderstood,
but seldom forgotten."
~19th Century English jurist~

~*~

"The hardest thing in the world to understand
is the income tax."
~Albert Einstein, physicist~

It Should Make You Furious

Did you know....

•　　Federal employee credit card programs were designed to save money. Rather than weaving through a lengthy procurement process to acquire basic supplies, federal employees could purchase job-related products with credit cards that would be paid by their agency. What began as a smart way to streamline government has since been corrupted by some federal employees who have abused the public trust.

A recent audit revealed that employees of the Department of Agriculture (USDA) diverted millions of dollars to personal purchases through their government-issued credit cards. Sampling 300 employees' purchases over six months, investigators estimated that 15 percent abused their government credit cards at a cost of $5.8 million. Taxpayer-funded purchases included Ozzie Osborne concert tickets, tattoos, lingerie, bartender school tuition, car payments, and cash advances.

The USDA has pledged a thorough investigation, but it will have a huge task:

55,000 USDA credit cards are in circulation, including 1,549 that are still held by people who no longer work at the USDA.

• The Defense Department has uncovered its own credit card scandal. Over one recent 18-month period, Air Force and Navy personnel used government-funded credit cards to charge at least $102,400 for admission to entertainment events, $48,250 for gambling, $69,300 for cruises, and $73,950 for exotic dance clubs and prostitutes.

~Heritage Organization/Research/Budget/bg1840.cfm~

(Isn't life just wonderful?)

Chapter 13

The Small Business Program

"A tax loophole is 'something that benefits the other guy'. If it benefits you, it is tax reform."
~Russell B. Long, U.S. Senator~

The good Senator Long from Louisiana certainly had a point. He never met a "tax reform" that he didn't like, and the miniscule amount of income taxes that he paid on his rather substantial income as he amassed his fortune reflected that truism.

The Internal Revenue Service is rather particular about reporting income. The IRS's crude approach to income is that if you have income —of any kind — you must declare it. Under certain rare conditions, you may have income that doesn't have to be declared, but for the most part, the IRS wants everything reported. No matter the source. In fact, if you obtain the money legally or illegally, the IRS 'suggests' that you declare it. Actually, it's more than a suggestion; it's the rule.

The IRS is a collection agency, not a police agency. Even if the money is earned from drug sales, theft, embezzlement, prostitution, extortion or other unlawful methods, the IRS still requires only that all income be declared and the proper amount of taxes be paid on the income. Their concern is about the taxes, not the crime. You may recall that, in the recent past, organized crime leaders who could not be arrested for any other reason were convicted of tax evasion.

There was a 'law-abiding' bank-robber from Florida who did indeed file an income tax return listing his income from the banks that he had robbed. Whether or not he actually paid income taxes wasn't revealed, and it was only at his trial following his arrest that it came to the public's attention that he had listed his profession on his income tax return as a 'withdrawal specialist'.

True story. You can check it out.

I wonder if the judge took his compliance with the income tax filing regulations into consideration when he passed sentence.

~*~

The Self-Employed Tax Caper

One small part of the Internal Revenue Code deals with the self-employed individual. The requirement of reporting the income is that if the net income of a self-employed individual exceeds $400.00, the taxpayer must file an income tax return showing that income.

For the self-employed, sole proprietorships and most small businesses, that form is a Schedule 'C' attachment to the standard income tax form 1040. The form is to reflect the total income from which the allowed business expenses are deducted before taxes are computed.

Taxes must be paid on the remainder, and those taxes include self-employment taxes. Currently, in

101

2007, the self-employed tax alone is 15.4% of the amount. Should a taxpayer experience a net profit of $1,000.00, the taxpayer must pay income tax on that $1,000.00 and in addition pay $154.00 self-employment taxes.

The Code also provides that any losses experienced in self-employment may be used to reduce the amount of taxable income from other sources, including wages and investments. Thus a person employed full time and receiving a salary could reduce the taxes on that salary, providing that the taxpayer experienced a net loss in his self-employment.

The taxpayer would file a Schedule 'C' in order to receive the benefits of any losses. There is a requirement that the self-employed individual must be in the business 'for the purpose of making a profit'. If there is no profit motive, there is no business and expense deductions are not allowed. The question is the profit motive, and only the taxpayer knows that for certain. The rules are only somewhat lax, but there are many ways of demonstrating a 'profit motive' for the business.

The section of the IRS rules covering a small business is not precisely clear, but includes the following:

> "In determining whether you are carrying on an activity for profit, all the facts are taken into account. No one factor alone is decisive. Among the factors to consider are whether:
>
> 1.   You carry on the activity in a business-like manner,
> 2.   The time and effort you put into the activity

indicate you intend to make it profitable,

       3.   You depend on income from the activity for your livelihood,

       4.   Your losses are due to circumstances beyond your control (or are normal in the start-up phase of your type of business),

       5.   You change your methods of operation in an attempt to improve profitability,

       6.   You, or your advisors, have the knowledge needed to carry on the activity as a successful business,

       7.   You were successful in making a profit in similar activities in the past,

       8.   The activity makes a profit in some years, and the amount of profit it makes, and

       9.   You can expect to make a future profit from the appreciation of the assets used in the activity."

As you can readily discern, there is a lot of leeway and a lot of flexibility in these few rules. Different people may read them in a different fashion, but I always chose to interpret them to the benefit of my clients. And my clients were always appreciative. Not one of those with whom I was working objected.

103

It was at this time I came up with what I considered a brilliant plan.

Andy had joined a multi-level marketing company by the name of Amway. And I joined as well. I've sure that every single one of you have heard about that organization. Andy had asked me to attend one of the meetings. I agreed. And I quickly saw the enormous income potential. It was, and still is, the easiest way to making a lot of money. That is, if one understands the true route, which requires only minimum participation, and follows it and encourages the ones that join with him or her to do the same. The method is quite easy, and not expensive, yet very few actually realize how the system works and therefore fail to achieve any level.

But, this isn't a sales pitch about Amway or any other similar multi-level marketing plan, so I won't get into the precise details of how anyone can make money at this time. Still, I saw a way to use the income tax program and Amway to reach a high-income level and a high-involvement level, and that was just what I wanted.

Everyone, and I do mean virtually everyone, knows several other people, speaks with them on the telephone, visits with them, and associates with a large number of people. One requirement of Amway is to recruit others in one's 'down-line', and if one knows people in a resort area or favorite vacation area, so much the better. I personally had relatives in Europe, and guess what? Amway reaches into Europe. And Mexico. And to the Caribbean, as well.

It is a business necessity that a recruiter visits his 'down-line' to help them build their business (recruit other people) by instructing and accompanying the down-line member on recruiting visits.

It is a fact that the IRS considers Amway a business, albeit reluctantly. It is a fact that travel expenses <u>for business purposes</u> are deductions against income.

You may well guess where this led. The only problem that I could see was that my client may not have realized that he was actually in business at the time he took a vacation trip, and that the purpose of the trip should have been to recruit a down-line member at that location. The trip would have become a business trip, with a few days of personal pleasure. The days of personal pleasure would not have been deductible, but the cost of the trip and the time spent recruiting would have been.

Frankly, you would have been astonished at the substantial number of people who instantly decided they had actually been on a business trip and had in fact tried to recruit a down-line while on the trip. Even long-distance calls to relatives had actually been made for the purpose of recruiting. The only fly in the ointment was that often the trips had been made before actually becoming a business partner in Amway. Still, that fact was easily glossed over. Clients were encouraged to only list the costs of trips actually made, but no verification was required and it is easily imaginable that many of my clients may have exaggerated slightly in the numbers that we provided in the income tax return.

Duh.

And most of these people actually did join Amway. Sort of like getting married after the child arrives, isn't it?

In truth, I was aware that many, even most, of those 'business trips' took place only in the mind of the client. Still, that didn't deter us from preparing the Schedule 'C' reflecting the write-offs.

You may also have been surprised at the fact that not one single client ever demurred. In fact, many clients were disappointed if it was necessary that they had to pay any income tax at all. Still, my efforts were to keep the lid on, so that the numbers wouldn't become blatantly obvious. That would attract the attention of the Internal Revenue Service snoops, and actually did attract such attention, as you will learn when you read my autobiography near the end of this recital.

Clients were also encouraged to keep receipts, receipts for everything. If one went to the grocery store and purchased a pencil, keep the receipt. If one had lunch or a fast-food burger, keep the receipt. If one went to dinner with a spouse or with friends, keep a receipt. And, of course, they did.

NOT!

And this caused no end of trouble when Kyle became involved at a later time.

Few clients, if any, maintained any sort of record or retained any sort of receipt, so if an audit were to occur, the business deductions would be denied. That wouldn't be too bad, I thought. The worst the client would have to do would be to pay the additional tax and there was a possibility that as long as the client insisted he or she was in business, some of the expenses would be allowed. A win-win situation, you know.

Didn't quite work out that way, 'best laid plans of mice and men....' but that's another matter that you will learn about later.

~*~

It was sometime after this period that I met Kyle, and we entered the next phase of preparing income tax returns with maximum write-offs.

Don't You Wish?

~*~

(A fable based on facts)

Dear IRS:

Enclosed is my tax return and payment. Please take note of the attached article from the USA Today newspaper. In the article, you will see that the Pentagon is paying $171.50 for hammers and NASA has paid $600.00 for a toilet seat.

Please find enclosed four toilet seats (value $2400) and six hammers (value $1029).

This brings my total payment to $3429.00. Please note the overpayment of $22.00 and apply it to the "Presidential Election Fund," as noted on my return. Might I suggest, you the send the above mentioned fund a 1.5-inch screw. (See attached article - **HUD paid $22.00 for a 1.5 inch Phillips Head Screw.**)

It has been a pleasure to pay my tax bill this year, and I look forward to paying it again next year. I just saw an article about the Pentagon and screwdrivers.

Sincerely,

Bill Jackson

(I would have, if only I had the nerve.)

Chapter 14

Small Corporations

Another section of the Internal Revenue Service Code deals with corporations. Corporations, as a rule, earn income and pay taxes on that income. The profits are then distributed to the stockholders and the stockholder includes that income on his or her income tax return and pays taxes. In effect, double taxation.

There is a provision in the Code, Regulation Section 1361(B) that allows a corporation with less than 54 stockholders and certain other limitations to file for Sub-Chapter S status. Under this election, the corporation chooses to be treated as a partnership. Partnerships do not pay federal income taxes, and thus a Sub-Chapter S Corporation would avoid paying income taxes. The profits are passed through to the stockholders to be included on their income tax returns. In this manner, the income is only taxed once.

Another quirk of the IRS operations was that, at the time, small corporations were seldom if ever audited. An obvious move would be to encourage the client to incorporate as a Sub-Chapter S Corporation, and thereby almost eliminate the chance of an audit. Needless to say, there were many conversions from self-employed to corporations. The fees for filing corporation income tax returns were substantially more than the fees for filing a Schedule C. And, naturally, I became adept at filing for incorporation in multiple states.

~*~

There were additional advantages to using a corporation rather than self-employed. The major area of those advantages was in the expenses that the corporation could pay for an officer or an employee or a director. Further, the Congress and the courts have decided that certain income should not be taxable to the individual and does not have to be reported as income.

In brief, certain payments may be made by the corporation is a deduction to the corporation, but is not income to the tax-filer. If the tax-filer can divert much of his income to flow through a corporation, it is possible to reduce taxes drastically. If the corporation does not have income to pay its obligations, in certain instances, the tax-filer can lend money to the corporation. The corporation has a loss, which, again under certain circumstances, may be passed legally along to the tax-filer, thus reducing his or her taxable income. Should such a transfer not be allowed legally, it is nonetheless transferred, albeit illegally. Even so, the odds of the IRS discovering such a transaction has been slight in the past, and is still unlikely today.

I won't bore you with a complete laundry list of the expenses that a corporation can make on behalf of the tax-filer, that you can easily find, but a few stand out from the rest.

1)   Hospital premiums, including premiums for supplementary medical insurance (Medicare) are excludable from the taxable income of an employee, an officer or a director of the corporation.

111

For example, you have set up a small corporation and have a substantial amount of income. You could hire your parents at a token salary and give them certain benefits, including the hospital premiums and the Medicare insurance premiums. Your parents would not have to report those payments and the corporation could write them off as an expense.

Children may also be covered under a dependent medical plan policy.

2)   Group life insurance premiums on term policies of $50,000 per employee may be a benefit for all employees, and both corporate officers and corporate directors may be considered employees, regardless of age.

3)   Accident and Health Plans may be offered to the employees, reducing the corporation's net (taxable) income without increasing the tax liability of the employee.

4)   Meals and lodging done for the convenience of the corporation may be paid by or reimbursed by the corporation without being reported on the tax-filer's tax return.

5)   The corporation can adopt a 'Cafeteria' plan that pays for both prescription and non-prescription medicines.

6)   Payments for education are a deduction for the corporation and are not reported by the tax-filer.

7)   Sale and continued use of residence. The tax-filer sells his house to his corporation. The corporation then becomes liable for the payment, taxes, insurance, utilities and maintenance. The tax-filer would occupy the residence, managing it on behalf of the corporation and. in as much as it was a part of his employment, would not report the free-living arrangement as income. If the tax-filer met certain

conditions, i.e. he or she was age 55 or older before the date of sale, had owned and lived in the property sold, and had not excluded gain on the sale of a home after July 20, 1981, then the tax-filer could earn a profit on the sale. The profit would not be taxable.

For example, you paid $100,000 for your home. The home is now worth $150,000. You could sell the house to the corporation for $200,000 and you would not pay tax on the $100,000 gain you experienced.

The corporation would have a $200,000 house that it would depreciate and would have a debt to you, if the corporation didn't have sufficient funds on hand to pay the entire transaction.

The end result would be that the corporation would have reduced its net income, and you would have $100,000 tax-free income.

~*~

There are a lot of other means of reducing the net, taxable income of a corporation, and, in fact, few of the corporations owned by tax-filers actually wind up with a profit. If it does report a profit, someone somewhere made a mistake. As an aside, Ford Motor Company, General Motors, and many other major well-known and famous corporations did not suffer the indignity of making a profit. So, my clients were in good company.

One of the means of reducing that income was deducting travel expenses.

The IRS auditors were becoming sticky about travel. However, I reasoned that if the corporation should pay for the travel, there would be no question that the expense was for business purposes. In fact, if the individual would lease his vehicle to the corporation, not only could a percentage of the cost of

113

operating the vehicle be taken, but also the entire cost could be shielded under the corporate structure.

A second opportunity was that a payment to family members for cleaning, maintenance, etc. could be made, provided that the entire house were to be leased to the corporation. A rental agreement would allow the corporation to lease the house and provide living space to the taxpayer in return for his or her maintaining the security of the structure. The corporation would pay utilities as well. And, yes, that would include Internet and cable television.

This procedure was much simpler and easier than trying to take a percentage of the house and the expenses and assigning that percentage to the business. Additionally, there was much less difficulty with the IRS, as there were no personal deductions for an in-home business.

A medical reimbursement plan could be established, allowing the corporation to pay for all health insurance and medical treatments. These expenses would also include travel to obtain medical care, and perhaps a 'rest break' from the difficulty of the work.

Educational expenses for employees of the corporation would allow the taxpayer to have the corporation pay for the children's education, including summer camp, golf camp, horse-back riding lessons, etc. Included would be lodging at places in order to obtain that education.

An additional deduction could be taken for a retirement plan. A retirement plan, properly prepared and adopted, would allow the tax-filer to set aside a part of his income to be taxed at a later time when the tax-filer may be taxed at a lower rate. Similar to a 401(K) plan, except in this instance the corporation would fund the entire retirement plan, the corporation could set up a SEP (Simplified Employee Pension) plan for each employee. By making the spouse an officer or a director, and by making any children members of the board, a retirement plan could be set up for each of the members of the family. As a norm, the tax-filer is the CEO of the business, and as CEO is responsible for the investing of the retirement funds, which could include loans to the officers/directors at some low interest rate.

In most occasions, the funding of all of these benefits would cause the Sub-Chapter S Corporation to experience a net operating loss. The IRS rules state that any profit must be assigned to the taxpayer and he must pay taxes on that income. Conversely, any loss is also assigned to the taxpayer and may be used to offset taxes on other income. The difference may often be significant. A client that made too much money to qualify for the earned income tax credit may well have qualified, after deducting the losses of the Sub-Chapter S Corporation.

Frankly, at the time, it seemed to be almost too good to be true, but that is what I read in the Internal Revenue Service Code, and what I used as a large part of my business consulting. My advice to individuals was to become involved in a Sub-Chapter S corporation or even a regular corporation or LLC, either one that they created for themselves or with someone else. If the corporation, through bad management and poor accounting, made a profit, they would just have to pay taxes on the profit. If the corporation had a loss, which virtually every business of any kind experiences the first few years, then the loss would offset other income.

An honest mistake that I must admit that I made at the time was being unaware that there are limits set on Sub-Chapter S corporations. I had created several Sub-S Corporations and as the result of

115

organizational expenses, had suffered the loss of a goodly sum of money. I allowed a few select tax clients to invest in those corporations with the result that the losses of the corporation would be prorated to the stockholders, and would allow my clients to substantially reduce their taxes. There was a slight flaw in this reasoning, but to be frank, this matter failed to come to the IRS's attention. At least, not until I committed errors in other areas.

Would you believe that some of my more knowledgeable and greedy clients actually had me form such a corporation just so they could write off personal expenses and reduce the amount of taxes they had to pay?

Really.

It's true.

It Should Make You Furious

"Puffing on My Top Hat, Tying up My White Tie"

Years of financial mismanagement have left the District of Columbia's government bankrupt and D.C. officials coming to Congress for yet another taxpayer bailout of hundreds of millions of dollars. So serious is the shortfall that clinics for the poor have been closed, teachers furloughed, snow covered streets unplowed, and police cars left un-repaired. But despite the fiscal crisis, Lloyd Arrington, Jr., President of the city-funded Economic Development Finance Corporation (EDFC), was able to maintain most of his costly perks despite the poor performance of the EDFC. Created in 1986 to encourage business development in the District of Columbia, and provided with $6.75 million in funds to lend to promising businesses, the EDFC and its wholly owned subsidiary, the Neighborhood Economic Development Corporation, made only 17 loans through 1994, or less than two loans per year. Although nine were in default or charged off as of 1994, the audit, reported that EDFC's President Arrington received a bonus of $17,000 on top of his $70,000 salary, another $1,650 to pay for parking, and $600 in "improper expenditures" for rented formal wear, dinners, and entertainment.

118

Nonetheless, the audit does indicate that progress toward fiscal restraint is being made: The EFDC's annual spending on flowers, which had hit a high of more than $2,000 per year in 1989 and 1990, had been phased out to zero by 1993.

Who's in Charge: City Council of the District of Columbia, (202) 724-8176.

Comic Relief?

~*~

Called in for an audit, Mr. Briggs was confronted by a surly IRS agent. "It says here, Mr. Briggs, that you are a bachelor; yet you claim a dependent son. Surely this must be a mistake."

Looking him straight in the eye, Mr. Briggs replied, "Yup, it surely was."

~**~

Simplified Tax Form

1040 EZ2DO TAX FORM

---

1. How much money did you make? $_____

2. Send it to us.   **Total:** $_____

U.S. Gov't. Form 89965309

~Unknown taxpayer~

Chapter 15

Trusts

In the State of North Carolina as in most states, an attorney is normally retained to form a trust. A little known fact is that an individual can form a trust for himself. And the trust is just as valid as if an attorney formed it.

Foreign trusts are also available to those who want to research the matter. Both foreign and domestic trusts may well be valid, expensive and legal, yet the use of the trust in income tax matters often surpass the benefits available through the Sub-Chapter S Corporation.

Trusts are often used to conceal the true owners of assets and income, as well as to shield assets. Wealthy individuals, small business owners, and professionals such as doctors and lawyers most often use trusts as vehicles to reduce or eliminate income taxes.

Income from a Sub-Chapter Corporation is subject to the 15.4% self-employment taxes, while a trust may often be exempt from the self-employment taxes, provided that any income or profit is properly handled. Another technique reduces or eliminates gift and estate taxes, enabling the taxpayer to pass his property to another without taxation.

122

There are two types of trust. One is the Foreign Trust and the second, a Domestic Trust. In each case, there are two genres.

First, there is the revocable trust, also known as the Living Trust or the Lifetime Trust. In this genre of trust, the maker of the trust may change the beneficiaries, the trustees or the terms of the trust. There is a danger. The Internal Revenue Service has successfully argued in court that a revocable trust dissolves upon the death of the maker, and the assets of the trust revert back to the maker's estate. Courts have also ruled that if the maker of the trust can alter the terms of the trust, there is no protection against creditor and that the maker of the trust can dissolve the trust at will. In short, the Judge can require that the trust's assets be sold to satisfy a debt against the maker of the trust.

The second genre is the Irrevocable Trust. An irrevocable trust is exactly as it is stated. Once the trust is set up and the Trustee is established, a Trustee other than the maker of the trust, the Trustee has complete and total control of the trust and its assets. The maker of the trust cannot benefit from the trust, nor can the maker of the trust require anything of the Trustee. This trust places considerable emphasis on the correctness of the selection of the Trustee, as all assets that are conveyed to the Trust are beyond the control of the maker of the trust. (Except under certain circumstances, which we will explore later.)

The Foreign Trust Program created to minimize taxes usually involves a series of trusts and International Business Companies (IBC's) usually formed in a foreign country. The trusts are vertically layered and two of the trusts are domestic trusts. The Trustee of each of the Trusts is an IBC that is formed in the foreign country.

123

The domestic trusts would be formed in the state where the tax-filer is living. The tax-filer turns his or her business over to the domestic trusts. One of the trusts would be the business trust that is in charge of the daily operations, including receiving income and paying expenses. This trust would file the business trust tax return (IRS Form 1041) reporting all income and all deductions.

The second domestic trust would be the equipment trust. All equipment belonging to the maker would be placed in the trust, including personal automobiles and even personal residences. The Equipment Trust would lease the equipment to the Business Trust at some agreed upon dollar amount, often highly inflated. Most, if not all, of the profits earned in the Business Trust's operating of the business would be drained into the Equipment Trust. The Equipment Trust would also file a trust tax return, or Form 1041.

The Equipment Trust distributes the income it receives to Foreign Trust-One through distributions, invoices and other means, which nullifies any tax due on the Equipment Trust tax return.

Foreign Trust-One then distributes all or most of its income to Foreign Trust-Two. Foreign Trust-One, because it has income from the United States, must file the US Form 1041, but since all or most of its income flows through to Foreign Trust-Two, the transfer nullifies any taxes due on Foreign Trust-One's income.

As all of Foreign Trust-Two's income is foreign-based, there is no United States IRS filing requirements.

Once the assets and/or income are in Foreign Trust-Two, a bank account is opened in the name of the Trust or an IBC, on which the tax-filer is a signatory. The trust documentation and the business records make it appear that the tax-filer is no longer in control of his or her business or its assets.

In as much as the tax-filer has no control and no income from the businesses, the tax-filer does not have any income to include in his or her tax return. Nor can any creditor attack the Trust for debts owed by the tax-filer.

The reality is that nothing has changed. The tax-filer still exercises full control over his or her business and assets.

Using the tax haven of Panama, to have a foreign trust formed there by a Panamanian lawyer costs about one thousand five hundred dollars per trust. The International Business Company is frequently formed in the same country, and the fee is approximately two thousand dollars, which includes some five hundred dollars paid to the Panamanian government as an incorporation fee. The attorney, or someone in his office, serves as the registered agent that serves as a local contact to file the annual documents required.

Panama, like Belize and the Bahamas, allows the stock of the IBC to be issued to 'Bearer', which conceals the true ownership of the IBC, which is the Trustee of all of the trusts. Some of the more discriminating clients would have one IBC formed to be the trustee of only one trust, thus eliminating another thread that links all of the trusts together.

Income received in one trust would be distributed to the other trust(s) by the way of rental agreements, fees for services, purchase and sale agreements and distributions. In many cases, the use of a little judicious bookkeeping and appraisals would result in little or no taxes.

125

An equipment or service trust was formed to hold equipment that is rented or leased to the business trust. The business trust reduced its income by claiming deductions for payment to the equipment trust, which is normally a foreign trust.

The family residence trust holds the family residences and furnishings, which are rented back to the taxpayer. The trust deducts depreciation and the expenses of maintaining and operating the residence, including gardening, pool service and utilities.

The business trust involves the transfer of the business into the trust. The business provides company vehicles, retirement plans, medical reimbursement provisions and other benefits in a manner much like the Sub-Chapter S Corporation.

Trusts are required to file income tax returns, and the fees we charged for trust tax returns were comparable to corporation fees. After receiving a letter from the North Carolina Bar Association that informed me I should cease creating trusts, I made certain that each client understood that it was the client himself who was forming the trust, not I; an act permissible under the North Carolina law. Of course, that didn't make the lawyers happy, but my clients were able to save substantial legal fees, which made my fee for 'reasonable' services more affordable.

While it is a certainty that most of my 'trust' clients reduced the amount of taxes they had to pay, a major purpose of the trust was asset protection. By forming a non-revocable trust, the controls of all assets are truly turned over to a trustee. If the taxpayer is not a trustee or a beneficiary, he or she has no control over the assets and those assets cannot be seized by anyone acting against the taxpayer. The estate is protected. The trustee could reach an irrevocable management agreement with an outside source, which might just be the taxpayer.

If the client has a business or a Sub-Chapter S Corporation and the stock or assets of the business is transferred to the trust, any income generated in the trust is subject to taxation. That is, after all deductions. Some trustees would hire a foreign corporation to provide services to the trust, and the funds transferred to that foreign corporation would be difficult to trace. That is especially true if that foreign corporation's ownership was vested in yet another foreign trust. If the foreign corporation or trust refuses to file an income tax return in the United States, the taxpayer can't be held responsible, can he?

Part of the Internal Revenue Service Code requires the disclosure of ownership in any foreign trust or corporation. And of course all United States citizens and tax filers are completely honest and will make full disclosure. And so are the preparers.

Right!

~ Points to Ponder ~

~*~

"The best measure of a man's honesty isn't his income tax return. It's the zero adjust on his bathroom scale." ~ Arthur C. Clarke, author~

~*~

"Taxes are not good things, but if you want services, somebody's got to pay for them so they're a necessary evil."
~Michael Bloomberg, Governor~

~*~

"Few of us ever test our powers of deduction, except when filling out an income tax form."
~Laurence J. Peter, author~

It Should Make You Furious

Did you know.....

- Medicare wastes more money than any other federal program, yet its strong public support leaves lawmakers hesitant to address program efficiencies, which cost taxpayers and Medicare recipients billions of dollars annually.

For example, Medicare pays as much as eight times what other federal agencies pay for the same drugs and medical supplies. The Department of Health and Human Services (HHS) recently compared the prices paid by Medicare and the Department of Veterans Affairs (VA) health care program for 16 types of medical equipment and supplies, which account for one-quarter of Medicare's equipment and supplies purchases. The evidence showed that Medicare paid an average of more than double what the VA paid for the same items. The largest difference was for saline solution, with Medicare paying $8.26 per liter compared to the $1.02 paid by the VA.

130

These higher prices not only cost the program more money, but also take more money out of the pockets of Medicare beneficiaries. In 2002, senior citizens' co-payments accounted for 20 percent of the $9.4 billion in allowed claims for medical equipment and supplies. Higher prices mean higher co-payments.

Medicare also overpays for drugs. In 2000, Medicare's payments for 24 leading drugs were $1.9 billion higher than they would have been under the prices paid by the VA or other federal agencies. Although Medicare is supposed to pay wholesale prices for drugs, it relies on drug manufacturers to define the prices, and manufacturers have strong incentives to inflate their prices.

Nor are inflated prices for drugs and supplies the most expensive examples of Medicare's inefficiencies. Basic payment errors—the results of deliberate fraud and administrative errors—cost $12.3 billion annually. As much as $7 billion owed to the program has gone uncollected or has been written off.[10] Finally, while Medicare contracts claims processing and administration to several private companies, 19 cases of contractor fraud have been settled in recent years, with a maximum settlement of $76 million.

Putting it all together, Medicare reform could save taxpayers and program beneficiaries $20 billion to $30 billion annually without

131

reducing benefits. That would be enough to fund a $3,000 refundable health care tax credit for nearly 10 million uninsured low-income households.

See the following:

Medicare Pays Inflated Prices for Equipment and Supplies

Markup	Item	*Price Paid By:*	
		Medicare	VA
751%	Saline Solution (1,000 ml)	$8.68	$1.02
538%	Nebulizer, with compressor	206.22	32.34
347%	Standard Wheelchair	570.68	127.72
130%	Semi-Electric hospital bed	1,754.55	762.10
240%	Commode chair	109.74	32.30

(Thousands of other examples, but you get the idea. And the shaft.)

....Source: Heritage Foundation/Research/Budget/bg1840

Chapter 16

The Offshore Operations Caper

William has been on my as...er.. my back. He explains that I am not being explicit enough, but I suppose that I believed I was boring everyone with details. Still, since he is recording all of this, and perhaps the readers do deserve a little more, so allow me to relate a complete occurrence. There are many variations to the Trust Program, one of which I will detail in the autobiography that I will relate in a short while.

The reader should be aware that everything in this operation is completely legal but was used for illegal purposes, and the reader should be warned that, if duplicated, use of this program could result in confrontation with the gargoyles of the Internal Revenue Service.

And, watch it! Those Federal guys and gals have no sense of humor, not any at all. Not when money is involved.

Well, let's set the stage. Suppose that your name is John, and that you have a substantial source of income, income that is from any source other than just W-2 wages. And let's use the offshore havens of Belize and Panama.

134

First, an International Business Company is set up for you in Belize. The Company, let's call it the ABC Company, is established and based in Belize and recorded in Belmopan, the Capital city of Belize. The requirement is there must be a registered agent in Belize to set up the Company and to file its annual report. Jim is a professional registered agent and is going to be our registered agent for a relatively small fee. He lives in Belize, and as a permanent resident or citizen Jim is acceptable to the Belize government. For the sum of one thousand five hundred dollars, he agrees to form the company, and for an additional two hundred and fifty dollars per year will serve as the Company's agent and file the annual report, which is a very minor, non-disclosure form. The annual fee to Belize for the Company is also paid, some three hundred dollars.

Your IBC Company is formed. The restrictions are that the Company can't conduct business inside the territorial limits of Belize, but may have an office in Belize to conduct business outside of the nation.

Why Belize? Simple, it's a tax haven. No income tax for International Business Companies (IBC's) and minor reporting data. This is also true in Panama and in other countries, but the underdeveloped country of Belize offers a safer environment than some of the others. The official language of the country is English. And the Belize Constitution requires a lot of proof if one is charged with money laundering. Tax evasion is not a crime in most of the tax-haven countries.

Once your Company is formed, a trust is also formed in Belize. The Belizean government requires only a written notice that a trust has been formed has to be recorded. Let's use the name 'Trust One' as the name of your first trust.

135

The stock of your ABC Company is issued to Trust One. In this manner, your Trust is the owner of the Company.

A second IBC is formed for you. As a name for the second IBC Company, let's use the name DEF Company.

DEF Company is the trustee of Trust One, which owns the stock of ABC Company. The beneficiary of Trust One is also the DEF Company.

A second trust is formed for you. Let's call it the Holding Trust. The stock of DEF Company is issued to the Holding Trust. DEF Company is also the Trustee of Holding Trust.

A third IBC, call it the GHI Company is created to the beneficiary of the Holding Trust. The stock of GHI Company is issued to 'Bearer'.

A bank account is opened in an offshore bank, the Provident Bank located in Belize City, Belize, in the name of ABC Company. Your source of income is assigned to ABC Company and the money is deposited into the bank account of ABC Company.

At this point, the money flows into the ABC Company's bank account. The ABC Company is owned by Trust One, which is in turn controlled by the DEF Company, who opens a bank account either in Belize or Panama. Excess funds are deposited into the second bank account, maintaining a working balance in the ABC Company bank account in the Provident Bank, Belize.

At this point, many individuals would have a Visa or Master Card debit card issued by Provident Bank and would use that card to withdraw cash at a bank in the United States.

The person trying to do this should be aware that the United States Government has successfully sued credit companies to force disclosure of offshore transactions by American citizens. See United States vs MasterCard, Visa, American Express, etc. Miami, Florida.

The use of multiple IBC's and shielding trusts avoid that disclosure requirement, and makes it extremely difficult for the Internal Revenue Service investigators to track the money, but the individual using the card is still subject to investigation if his or her lifestyle exceeds their income.

One little-known but effective method used is that the ABC Company would open a bank account in the United States. First, ABC Company would register as a foreign corporation, and would submit the proper documents to obtain a federal identification number. The records at the bank and the Social Security Department would reveal that the owner of the Company would be Trust One. There would be no record of any American citizen owning any part of the ABC Company, nor would there be any record of any American Citizen being the Trustee or the Beneficiary of Trust One.

One benefit of the ABC Company maintaining a bank account with the United States Bank is that wire transfer in each direction could send money, legitimately.

The US bank would issue a debit card to the ABC Company, which would be used by its agent, you.

A further precaution would be that you would become an employee, on a part-time basis, of the ABC Company on a minimum salary plus commissions. The Company would issue a W-2 with the appropriate F.I.C.A. and withholding, if any, on the minimum salary. In as much as the ABC Company had zero income from its United States operation, there would be no tax returns filed.

As an employee of the ABC Company, the Company could lend you money, as needed, and of course, repayment would be made, including interest.

The ABC Company, from its operational base in Belize, could invest in the United States Stock Exchange, or in foreign stock exchanges, and do other business. Because the ABC Company is a foreign entity, its income from operations outside of the United States would be exempt from US taxes.

With the home office of the ABC Company being in Belize, any trips taken by you to its home office, or any trips made on behalf of the Company to any section of the world for any reason, would be at the expense of the Company, which could reimburse you, tax free, for any expenses that you paid on behalf of the Company.

Did you follow all of that? Sounds extremely complicated, doesn't it? Well, it is. And deliberately so. If it were simple to follow and easy to trace, there would be no protection and no tax advantage. And no reason to retain someone like me.

Still, I will try to clarify much of this information in the autobiography that follows wherein I shall walk you through a complete transaction.

~ Points to Ponder ~

~*~

"If a person is an economic being and figures out the odds, then there is a very high incentive to cheat. That is, of course, putting aside honor, duty and patriotism."
~Jerome Kurtz, former Commissioner, Internal Revenue Service~

~*~

"Lord, the money we do spend on Government and it's not one bit better than the government we got for one third the money twenty years ago."
~Will Rogers, Humorist~

~*~

The wages of sin are death, but by the time taxes are taken out, it's just sort of a tired feeling."
~Comedian~

Chapter 17

International Business Company Caper

There certainly may be other less complicated and less expensive ways to use foreign countries and Internal Business Companies. One example is where the businessman tax-filer (note that throughout, I have used the expression 'tax-filer' as opposed to 'taxpayer'. Wonder why? Keep reading!) establishes an IBC in Panama or the Cayman Islands with the same exact name as that of his or her business. The IBC also has a bank account in that foreign country. As the tax-filer would receive checks from customers, the tax-filer sends the checks to the bank in the foreign country. The foreign bank then uses the correspondent bank account in the United States to process the checks so it would never appear to the payer, upon reviewing the canceled check, that the payment was sent offshore. Once the checks clear, the tax-filer's IBC account is credited for the check payments.

The stock of the IBC is issued to 'Bearer', making it virtually impossible for anyone to determine who is the owner of the IBC. The result is that the money has been transferred to the tax haven jurisdiction. The use of debit cards issued by the foreign bank to withdraw funds helps insure the privacy of the tax-filer.

~*~

Another tax reduction program involved the use of invoices for billing. An IBC would be set up in either Belize, Nevis, Panama or the Bahamas. Once again, the stock would be issued in the name of 'Bearer'. A nominee—usually an agent paid by the tax-filer—would manage the IBC. A bank account would be opened under the name of the International Business Company and the tax-filer would be listed as a signatory on the account. The 'Manager' would issue invoices to the tax-filer's businesses for goods purchased by the tax-filer. The tax-filer then sends payment to the IBC that gets deposited into the bank account of the IBC. The tax-filer also takes a business deduction for the payment to the IBC, with the result that his or her taxable income is reduced and therefore less income tax is paid.

Once again, a debit card enables the tax-filer to withdraw funds at any US bank.

~*~

Although I have covered the subject, to enable the reader to totally comprehend the process, a short description of how the tax-filer would access funds from foreign banks follows.

Credit/Debit Cards. Once the bank account is established in a foreign bank, that bank issues a bankcard. Sometimes the card is a debit card, which drafts money directly from the bank account to pay for a purchase or a withdrawal. At other times the bank

143

will issue credit cards, on which monthly installment payments could be made. Either of the cards could also be used to pay for everyday expenses.

Loans. The tax-filer's IBC would make a loan to the tax-filer. The funds would be wire transferred from the IBC's bank account to the tax-filer's U.S. bank account. Since these wired funds are loans, they are not taxable. If the ownership of the IBC is through bearer shares, it is very difficult for anyone to determine if the loan is legitimate or not. Preparing loan documents that are signed by the tax-filer in favor of the IBC makes the loan seem legitimate, and only the tax-filer knows for sure.

.

It Should Make You Furious

Did you know....

• In 2002, the Department of Education received an application to certify the student loan participation of the Y'Hica Institute in London, England. After approving the certification, the department received and approved student loan applications from three Y'Hica students and disbursed $55,000.

The Education Department administrators overlooked one problem: Neither the Y'Hica Institute nor the three students who received the $55,000 existed. The fictitious college and students were created (on paper) by congressional investigators to test the Department of Education's verification pro-cedures. All of the documents were faked, right down to naming one of the fictional loan student applicants "Susan M. Collins," after the Senator requesting the investigation.

Such carelessness helps to explain why federal student loan programs routinely receive poor management reviews from government auditors. At last count, $21.8 billion worth of student loans are in default, and too many cases of fraud are left undetected. Tracking students across federal programs, verifying loan application data with IRS income data, and

146

implementing controls to prevent the disbursement of loans to fraudulent applicants could save taxpayers billions of dollars.

~ Heritage
Foundation/Research/Budget~

Comic Relief?

~*~

"The more you earn, the less you keep,
And now I lay me down to sleep.
I pray the Lord my soul to take,
If the tax collector hasn't got it before I wake.
~Ogden Nash~

~*~

A taxpayer was ordered in for an audit of his recent returns. He showed up with all his financial records, then sat for what seemed like hours watching the IRS accountant pore over the numbers.

Finally the agent looked up. "You must be a tremendous fan of Sir Arthur Conan Doyle," he said.

"Why would you say that?", the taxpayer asked.

"You've made more brilliant deductions on your last three tax returns than Sherlock Holmes made in his entire career."

~Edgar Bergen, Ventriloquist and Comedian~

Chapter 18

The Donations to Charity Caper

The Internal Revenue Code (or IRC) (more formally, the 'Internal Revenue Code of 1986, as amended') is the main body of domestic statutory tax law of the United States. The IRC is published as title 26 of the United States Code (USC), and is also known as the internal revenue title.

The Internal Revenue Code of 1939 cracked the door open, the Internal Revenue Code of 1954 further opened the door, and the Internal Revenue code of 1986 swung the door wide open. Section 2 of the Tax Reform Act of 1986 provides (in part): "to the Internal Revenue Code of 1986 shall include a reference to the provisions of law formerly known as the Internal Revenue Code of 1954."

For our current purposes, we are concerned with Title 26: Internal Revenue Code, Subtitle A: Income Taxes – Chapter 1: Normal Taxes and Surtaxes – Subchapter B: Computation of Taxable Income – Part VI: Itemized Deductions for Individuals and Corporations.

To the general public, what this all means is that Title 26 deals with, among other things, itemized deductions for the individual or business, and among those deductions are contributions to charities and churches.

Section 170(c) of the Internal Revenue Code permits a tax-filer that itemizes his or her deductions to list among the deductions contributions to certain charities and religious organizations. The amount of contributions that can be deducted is limited to fifty percent of the adjusted gross income of the tax-filer. If the tax-filer had an adjusted gross income of $150,000.00, the tax-filer could transfer one-half, or $75,000.00 to an acceptable non-profit or charitable organization with the result that the taxable income would be reduced by $75,000.00.

A non-exhaustive list of organizations that are likely to be approved by the Internal Revenue Service as a tax deductible charity includes Synagogues, churches and other religious organizations; a fraternal order or lodge; an organization of war veterans, public charities and private charities.

To simply donate money to approved organizations under this program would mean that the tax-filer has given away his money, when the real intent of the tax-filer is to keep his money and not pay taxes. What better way than to have his or her own tax-exempt non-profit organization?

It is simple to create such an organization. A person forms a corporation or a limited liability company under the restrictions of the state of residence. For the most part, individual states have virtually the same requirements for forming a corporation. Virginia, North Carolina, South Carolina, Tennessee and Maryland have almost identical requirements, as does New Jersey. Some of the states allow corporations to be formed on-line, reducing the amount of driving or mail necessary to form corporations in different states.

After the organization has been formed, submissions are made to the Internal Revenue Service

151

for designation as a 501 (c) (3) tax-exempt non-profit status.

Section 501 (c) (3) is just one of the tax law provisions granting exemption from the federal income tax to non-profit organizations. The exemptions apply to corporations and any community chest, fund, or foundation, organized and operated exclusively for religious, charitable, scientific, testing or public safety, literary, or to foster national or international amateur sports competition, or for the prevention of cruelty to children or animals.

Some organizations automatically acquire 501 (c) (3) status upon filing proper documents. An example is the filings of the articles of incorporation as a church. Other types of organizations are more likely to be required to submit additional documentation and undergo further scrutiny, with result that individuals looking to minimize their taxes are more apt to choose a church as the not-for-profit vehicle.

The particular section that interests most tax-filers is 26 U S C 170 that provides a deduction, for federal income tax purposes for donors who make charitable contributions to most types of 501 (c) (3) organizations.

Subsequent to the approval of the IRS having been granted, donations to that organization are deductible for the donor, providing that the donor itemizes his or her deductions on the federal tax return.

The tax-filer then becomes a director, an employee, a consultant or a volunteer with the Non-Profit Organization (NPO). Perhaps even the only director, etc., or perhaps other members of his family or circle of friends may become involved with the NPO.

The non-profit organization can then pay for or reimburse certain expenses incurred by the tax-filer.

Benefits such as health insurance, travel expenses, entertainment and other ordinary personal expenses are often paid for by the tax-exempt NPO.

In this manner, the tax-filer obtains the deduction, but is able to use much of the money for personal benefits that has the semblance of legality.

And churches are even better.

It Should Make You Furious

Did you know.....

•   The Army Corps of Engineers spends $5 billion annually constructing dams and other water projects. Yet, in a massive conflict of interest, it is also charged with evaluating the science and economics of each proposed water project. The Corps' "strategic vision" calls on managers to increase their budgets as rapidly as possible, which requires approving as many proposed projects as possible. Consequently, the Corps has repeatedly been accused of deliberately manipulating its economic studies to justify unworthy projects.

Investigations by the GAO, *The Washington Post*, and several private organizations have found that Corps studies routinely contain dozens of basic arithmetic errors, computer errors, and ridiculous economic assumptions that artificially inflate the benefits of water projects by as much as 300 percent. In one case, a study's authors inflated a project's benefits by using a 2.5 percent interest rate that dated back to 1954. In many cases in which the Corps calculated that a project would be a net benefit, arithmetic

154

corrections revealed that the costs would be many times greater than the benefits. By that point, of course, the unnecessary and wasteful project is often underway and cannot be stopped; these errors appear to reflect more deception than sloppiness. A *Washington Post* investigation uncovered managers ordering analysts to "get creative," to "look for ways to get to yes as fast as possible," and "not to take no for an answer." After a public outcry, in 2002, the Corps suspended work on 150 projects to review the economics used to justify them. However, given the combination of Congress's thirst for pork-barrel projects and the Corps' built-in incentives to approve projects that will increase its budget, real reforms seem unlikely.

~ Heritage Foundation/Research/Budget/bg1840~

Chapter 19

The "Old Time Religion' Caper

One of – if not the – most used (and misused) choices of the experienced tax-filer seeking to avoid taxation is the formation of a church. With the proliferation of sects of religion, and even non-religion, it is only a matter of completing the proper paperwork to have a recognized, affiliated church with one splinter group or another. In the absence of such an affiliation, it is also rather easy to form a sect independent of all others. There are very few requirements on the state level as to the filings of the papers to organize a church, and may be established in a matter of weeks.

There are certain characteristics that the Internal Revenue Service looks for in any application by a church for the automatic 501 (c) (3) status. Let's discuss a few.

(1) Distinct legal existence. Simply saying "I Am A Church" is no longer acceptable. However, the expenses and the amount of work to prepare 'Articles of Incorporation of the ......Church' is minimal. The adoption of the Articles constitutes proof of the distinct legal existence of the church.

(2) Recognized creed and form of worship. Either adopting an existing creed or simply publishing a creed based on any obscure religious principle will qualify.

(3) Definite and distinct ecclesiastical government. Establishing a 'Council of Elders' fills the requirement.

(4) Formal code of doctrine and discipline. And

(5) Distinct religious history. Use of the recognized religion of Christianity or any of the other forms of religion, including Islam is acceptable.

(6) Membership not associated with other churches. Cannot be member of more than one church. This requirement does not limit or eliminate visits to other churches or religious organizations.

(7) Organization of ordained ministers. Even if there is only one minister; or two, as husband and wife (or even young children) may each be a minister.

(8) Regular religious services, held in established places of worship. May include a garage or a spare room, if no other place is available.

(9) Schools for preparation of its members, its ministers and the young. Even if the school or schools only conducts classes or training on occasion or for brief periods of time.

Not all of these ingredients are needed to be a church, but the IRS will definitely look for several. Still, any reasonable person can see how easily the IRS requirements may be circumvented.

Let's look at a specific example.

A client, call him Joe, married with two children, resides in the city of Burlington, North Carolina. He is employed by a local business, and his salary is $95,000.00 per year. His wife, Jane, is also employed, as a registered nurse, and her salary is $55,000.00 per year. One child is 16 and the second one is 14. The family lives in a two-story, four-bedroom house, with an attached two-car garage. Joe and Jane pay, on an average, twenty-five thousand dollars to the federal government and six thousand dollars to the state of North Carolina. With other taxes, the total sum of taxes paid is equal to $37,000.00. The tax-filer decides that this is entirely too much money to pay to the United States Government and seeks ways to reduce his tax liability.

Joe and Jane decide to hire an attorney or a tax-wise promoter (like me) to establish a church in the state of North Carolina, to be located in Burlington, NC. A Board of Directors or Council of Elders is provided for in the Articles of Incorporation that creates the church. The requirements in the Articles set out a quorum required to hold a meeting of the Council or the Board, and that quorum is set at one. Thus the tax-filer, as a director or a member of the Council can hold a meeting of the organization with only one person present; himself.

Rather than starting his own religious sect, he opts to align his church with one of the numerous religious organizations. The sole requirement is that the tax-filer's church has to pay an annual assessment of one hundred and fifty dollars to the head organization. No other reporting or actions are required of the tax-filer's church.

Next, the Board sets up requirements for ordaining ministers. One of the requirements is that the would-be minister must attend the training school that will be conducted by the Board. In this instance, the school period was for four hours. As the only member of the Board, the tax-filer is also the instructor in the school. At that time, Joe includes his wife and two children, and counts himself as the fourth student.

After completion of the four hours of 'instruction', all four are ordained as ministers in the 'church'. The goal of the 'church' is to spread good will to all corners of the earth and all of its inhabitants. The reason the children were ordained as 'ministers' will

158

become apparent as we further uncover the tax-filer's operations.

Under expert tax advice, Joe and Jane file separate income tax returns during the following year. Each filer claims one of the children as a dependent, as neither of the two children have enough income to be required to file their own income tax return.

Joe donates twenty-five thousand dollars to the 'church'. In addition, he donates his personal vehicle, which is valued at twenty-two thousand five hundred dollars. The total of his donation amounts to forty-five thousand five hundred dollars. Without the donation, the tax-filer's income tax would amount sixty three percent of the thirty seven thousand dollars or to twenty-three thousand three hundred and ten dollars. Joe would not qualify for the automatic child tax credit of one thousand dollars, thus his federal tax liability would be $23,310. His North Carolina State tax would be three thousand four hundred and twenty-seven dollars and his total tax liability would be $26,737.

By making the donation to the church, Joe's taxable income drops to less than thirty seven thousand dollars. His income tax would amount to four thousand nine hundred and seventeen dollars. He would still not qualify for the one thousand dollars child tax credit and thus his federal income tax liability would remain $4,917. His North Carolina State Income tax would be one thousand two hundred and seventy, and his total income tax liability would be $6,241, a reduction of $20,496.00.

That is correct, he would pay twenty thousand four hundred and ninety six dollars less in income taxes. And Jane, his wife, following in the same footsteps would donate her automobile, valued at $20,000 and also donate $7,500 cash to the church. Without the donation, her federal taxes would be

159

$7,196.00. Jane would qualify for the $1,000 child tax credit and then her federal tax liability would be $6,196. Her North Carolina income tax would be $937 and therefore her total tax liability would be $7,133.00.

With the donation, Jane's federal income tax becomes $2,024 and with the $1,000 child tax credit, her federal liability becomes $1,024. Her North Carolina remains at $937 so her entire tax liability is $1,961, or a reduction of $5,172.00.

When one combines the $20,496 reduction in Joe's income taxes and $5,172 reduction in Jane's income taxes, for a total reduction of $25,668, a savings of over sixty-six percent, it is easy to understand why any knowledgeable person may choose to form his own religious organization.

Wait! There's more. It gets even better. But first, a commercial break.

160

~ Points to Ponder ~

~*~

"There may be liberty and justice for all, but there are tax breaks only for a few select."
~Martin A. Sullivan~

~*~

"The United States has a system of taxation by confession."
~Hugo Black~

~*~

"Thank God we don't get all the government we pay for."
~Will Rogers, Humorist~

Chapter 20

The Religious Conversion Caper

As I promised, there is more. And it only gets better and better. Here we sit with a church that has four ordained ministers; a minister, an assistant minister, and their two 'youth ministers'.

The church also owns two automobiles and has $32,500 in cash in the bank.

But the tax-filer wants the use of his money.

Under the Internal Revenue Code, there are certain payments that can be made to ordained ministers without becoming taxable income to the tax-filer.

First, the minister may be paid a housing allowance. That allowance is not taxable. Generally, the housing allowance includes rent, mortgage payments, repairs, gardening, pool maintenance and other expenses relating directly to providing a home. Included in those expenses may be the cost of cleaning the house, and in our case, the two junior ministers are paid two thousand dollars per year each to make sure the ministerial home is kept clean.

Second, the compensation that a church pays to its ministers in the exercise of the ministry is not subject to FICA taxes. The minister can and does apply for an exemption for the Self-Employment Contributions Act (SECA). This amounts to a 15.4% raise in annual compensation.

Third, the church can furnish full medical coverage to its ministers, including any insurance or Medicare premiums. These sums are also exempt from federal or state taxes.

The church adopts an Accountable Reimbursement Plan. Under the plan, the expense must involve a business connection, requires the employee to substantiate expenses incurred and to return any excess when funds are advanced.

One common business expense reimbursement is for automobile mileage. If the church or religious organization pays a mileage allowance at a rate that is equal to or less than the federal standard rate, the amount of the deduction has been deemed to be substantiated in accordance with the Internal Revenue Service regulations. The federal standard rate for mileage changes from one year to the next. There is no income or employment tax consequences to the reimbursed individual provided that the minister employee substantiates the time, place and business purposes of the automobile mileage for which reimbursement is sought. Of course, reimbursement for automobile mileage incurred for personal purposes is includible in the individual's income. Ha! As if any minister ever drove the church's vehicles on personal business, it was always on the church's business.

And it's much easer if the vehicle is actually owned by the church. Plus, the church may be exempt from local property taxes as well.

Other expenses that were reimbursable by the minister's church were meals and lodging as the minister and his fellow ministers traveled in wide circles, including Mexico and Cancun as well as Paris, London and Berlin, trying to convert 'non-believers' to the true faith.

Yeah!

165

Oh, by the way. Each of the ministers could have been paid a housing allowance, except there weren't enough funds to pay all four. Only three received the housing allowances, each one of two receiving $15,000 and the third receiving $2,500 and a church note for the balance. The fourth received a church note for the full amount. Of course, the church notes bore interest at the maximum amount allowed by law.

It Should Make You Furious

Did you know....

• The earned income tax credit (EITC) provides $31 billion in refundable tax credits to 19 million low-income families. The IRS estimates that $8.5 billion to $9.9 billion of this amount—nearly one-third—is wasted in overpayments.

The complexity of the EITC law leads to many of these mistakes. Calculating the credits is more complex than calculating regular income taxes. While the credit amount depends on the number of children in a household, the tax code does not clearly define how a child qualifies for the credit. In addition, fraud and underreporting of income are common, and the IRS lacks the resources to verify the qualifications of all EITC claimants

• Government's layering of new programs on top of old ones inherently creates duplication. Having several agencies perform similar duties is wasteful and confuses program beneficiaries who must navigate each program's distinct rules and requirements.

Some overlap is inevitable because some agencies are defined by *whom* they serve (e.g., veterans, Native Americans, urbanites, and rural families), while others are defined by *what* they provide (e.g., housing, education, health care, and economic development). When these agencies' constituencies overlap, each relevant agency will often have its own program. With 342 separate economic development programs, the federal government needs to make consolidation a priority.

Chapter 21

Foundations and Not-For-Profit Organizations

For those clients who didn't want to challenge God, or who didn't want to bother maintaining all of the records and requirements of establishing a church, it was simple to create a non-profit organization (NPO) of another type. The most popular would be to set up a non-profit corporation for educational pursuit and research. Once again, the paperwork would be completed to qualify the NPO as a Section 501 (c) (3). It would take a little longer and wasn't automatic as with a church, but the extended time period isn't that great.

Once the 501 (c) (3) status is granted, all donations made to that NPO become deductible for the tax-filer who itemized his or her tax return. Many tax-filers would donate as much as 35% of their income to the NPO and then would serve as a director or a trustee or other official of the NPO.

It was seldom that a salary of any significance would be paid to the tax-filer by the NPO. After all, he or she had donated the money to avoid paying taxes on that amount. The NPO, often a foundation, would pay for expenses for its director(s) to travel to various places in the pursuit of educational excellence.

One NPO was doing research on how long it would take an individual to play golf like a pro. The research required the official to travel to various golf courses in the United States and abroad, to determine the proper way to putt a ball on different types of grass. Over a period of several years, the NPO received almost $500,000.00 in donations and spent almost all of the money on expenses. The NPO did establish a retirement plan for its directors and funded that retirement plan to the tune of $20,000.00 per year. The educational research program was so attractive that fellow workers and relatives became directors of the NPO. (After having contributed substantial amounts, of course.)

~*~

Another educational NPO had three teenagers as its directors. The NPO sponsored all three for college, two to University of North Carolina at Chapel Hill and one to Notre Dame University. Tuition and living expenses were included, as was car allowances and miscellaneous expenses.

By the way, for your information, the Internal Revenue Service, because of the size of their charitable contributions, audited two people who had established non-profit organizations for educational purposes. In each case, not only were the deductions allowed, but further, the IRS found a couple of small errors, resulting in an additional refund of $350.00 to one person and $187.00 to the other.

~*~

Prevention of cruelty to animals or to children was also a purpose for which non-profit organizations were easily established. Like churches, the Internal Revenue Service readily approved foundations of this type as charitable organizations. Tax-filers who were also animal owners found the first purpose suited their needs and provided for care to their animals. With tax-deductible dollars, of course.

Foundations for the prevention of cruelty to children were a little more difficult for me to accept as a client. That was a subject about which I had strong personal feelings. In fact, I only know of one such foundation that was formed by an associate of mine, and the person who wanted the foundation to be created was himself very active in trying to protect young children from sexual predators. The director of the foundation, who is the spouse of the tax-filer, has been instrumental in trying to have a law known as 'Jessica's Law' enacted in multiple states. That law provides for much stronger punishments for sexual predators who cause children anguish.

~*~

Foundations, or non-profit organizations, have been created for a wide variety of purposes; study of art, music, geography; the list is almost endless. I would like to believe that some of the organizations we helped create did carry out their stated intent, however, I am certain that most of the non-profit organizations were only toys for well-educated tax-filers.

Or perhaps an unscrupulous tax preparer.

172

.

A Moment of Relaxation

~*~

What to Wear for IRS

A man who was called to testify at the IRS, asked his accountant for advice on what to wear. "Wear your shabbiest clothing. Let him think you are a pauper," the accountant replied.

Then he asked his lawyer the same question, but got the opposite advice. "Do not let them intimidate you. Wear your most elegant suit and tie."

Confused, the man went to his Rabbi, told him of the conflicting advice, and requested some resolution of the dilemma.

"Let me tell you a story," replied the Rabbi. "A woman, about to be married, asked her mother what to wear on her wedding night. 'Wear a heavy, long, flannel nightgown that goes right up to your neck.' But when she asked her best friend, she got conflicting advice. Wear your most sexy negligee, with a v-neck right down to your navel."

The man protested: "What does all this have to do with my problem with the IRS?"

The Rabbi replied, "No matter what you wear when you go to see the IRS, you are going to get screwed."

(Amen.)

Chapter 22

Autobiography

"A taxpaying public that does not understand the law is a taxpaying public that cannot comply with the law."
~Former IRS Commissioner Lawrence B. Gibbs, April 14, 1987~

And with these words, it's time to become somewhat serious about a difficult subject. Frankly, I'm surprised and somewhat grateful that you've made it this far. I'm sure that it hasn't been easy.

For those of you who have enjoyed the '~ Points to Ponder ~' and other intermissions and found humor in the irony, there are several pages at the end of this narrative for your reflections and for your amusements.

Now, though, it's the place to reveal the details of my life. I told you this time was coming, and it's now arrived. Perhaps you might find the reason that I was so willing to joust with the Internal Revenue Service dragon. You may also want to tune out at this point and jump to the humorous points at the end. I really wouldn't blame you. Not that the following is anything less than the truth, but frequently the truth is not only painful but also not very entertaining.

As much as anything, it was an affinity for numbers that I have had since I was a child that led me to the profession of preparing income tax returns.

No, no matter what the Internal Revenue Service investigators or the U.S. District Attorney may have claimed, I wasn't born to become a professional cheat. Although, the way it came about might lead anyone to presume it was my destiny.

There is no school that one attends to learn to falsify income tax returns. In fact, most preparers who bend the rules, or snap them in two, begin in the most minor way. Then, the situation seems to mushroom.

I've talked about two associates, William P. and Sanjiv. Shortly, I'll introduce you to the third, Kyle, who I have mentioned only briefly.

I will also take you through every step of how foreign trusts and international business companies are set up and utilized to minimize the tax bill, or to minimize it to an acceptable level.

As I have already mentioned, William P. is a black man from Winston Salem and Sanjiv is a Hindu from India. Kyle was American Indian mixed with Caucasian and Hispanic. He was from Eastern Texas. But, there'll be more about him later.

As for me, I guess that you could say that I was the "red-neck" of the group, coming from the hills of North Carolina near the Great Smoky Mountain range.

Like I said, I have an aptitude for numbers and all forms of mathematics were easy for me to learn. Thanks to a caring grandmother who, although having had only a small amount of education herself, wanted success for her favorite grandson. She began teaching me to read and to count as well as to add and subtract simple numbers long before I began school at the age of 5½.

For those of you who may not be aware, once upon a time there was a point in the past when kindergarten or preschool didn't exist. (Darn, don't

177

look now, but I'm getting to be an old man. Hell, I'm a very old man.)

During my early school years, I was especially proud of my mathematical talents and those talents allowed me to stand out a little in the classroom. This was very important to me, as it allowed me to impress the love of my life, Eula Mae W_____.

A short, blonde-headed, blue-eyed beauty, Eula Mae entered my life on the first day of school as I entered the first grade classroom. She dropped her books and I picked them up and handed them to her. She batted her gorgeous eyes at me, and said, "I didn't know you were my boy-friend."

Wow! I was smitten. And, of course, all I could do was stammer and stutter. (Mountain boys are mostly shy, especially when there are fifteen to twenty others around) Then, it was necessary to impress Eula Mae, and my math skills—we called it 'arithmetic'—became a strong part of my image. I really wanted to make a good impression.

Guess it didn't impress her too much. Just as my third year in school began, Eula Mae's parents moved to Polkville, North Carolina, taking my sunshine away. At the age of 7 ½, I suffered a complete heartbreak. Took me at least a week to get over it; I met Martha Sue, another blonde, blue-eyed classmate. Even so, I have never forgotten Eula Mae and often wonder what would, could have happened. (Yes, I did tell my fantastic wife of 48 years about Eula Mae)

My interest in mathematics was greatly stimulated by Mr. Wilson, from Mill Springs, North Carolina. He was a math whiz and had techniques of computing numbers that dazzled the mind. Again, this was before computers or even calculators becoming available to the public. Mr. Wilson's mind was fantastic and his trick methods of computing the sum of a long

178

column of numbers by cross adding were fascinating to an eager student. Being an excellent teacher, Mr. Wilson was more than wiling to share his knowledge with anyone who could understand and who really wanted to learn.

Because of these three individuals, I had developed a fondness for mathematics that I would use to earn a living during much of my adult life. Unfortunately for me, I didn't always use that small, God-given talent in the accepted and legal manner.

Being a child of the mountains and growing up in a wooded countryside, I did have a slight problem with discipline. Never disobeying a direct order from either my mother or my father and not a violent rebel, I was a rebel, nonetheless. For the most part, I suppose that I am aware that rules are necessary for an orderly society and that everyone should follow the rules. Including me.

On the other hand, I have only broken a rule when the rule began to interfere with attaining goals that I had set for myself. I wasn't willing to allow anything to deter me from my goals.

Often, as a child, the breech of rules led to an upset mother using a keen hickory switch on my bare legs. Switches that my mother would require me to bring to her, and if those switches weren't large enough, she would find another switch and then use them both.

That was acceptable; the punishment only hurt for a little while. The pain always faded long before the stripes the switches caused, and the stripes always faded long before the thrill and enjoyment of attaining the goal that I had accomplished.

And, besides, mountain boys don't cry.

One thing mountain boys do is have fun. Are you familiar with the type of trees that grow in the mountains? We referred to the slender trees as saplings; trees that were about twenty to thirty feet tall and quite limber.

Did you know that if you climb to the top of one of those trees and sway back and forward that you can gain enough momentum to swing from one tree to another? That is, provided that the tree doesn't break.

As kids – there were two boys and three girls – we would often climb those trees and pretend to be Tarzan, the Ape Man (or Jane); swinging from tree to tree.

One day, having conveniently ignored the call of Mother, my brother and I were high in the trees and having a lot of fun. One of the girls must have ratted us out. Mom appeared on the ground under us, demanding that we come down. She had a switch in her hand. And, it was a HUGE switch. When we declined the privilege of descending to punishment, Mom began climbing the tree after us. She didn't like to climb, but she was mad.

Of course, my brother and I began to sway the tree. Mom held on for dear life. She was petrified of high places. Brother and I escaped to another tree only to find that Mom was frozen in fear. Then we had to return to help Mom climb back down to the ground.

Think she was grateful? Whap. Whap. Whap. Better believe that she whipped my butt. I didn't forget that one for quite a while.

~*~

Mom wasn't especially strict, only punishing us when we violated one of her few rules, threatening us with telling Dad if we were too rowdy. Or if she caught us smoking one of the cigarettes we stole from her or dad.

180

Dad had been a professional boxer and a professional gambler. But he had another secret.

My daddy was a 'Moon Shiner.'

That's right; he helped make moonshine – illegal liquor, to those of you up North – in the hills of North Carolina. For those of you in the Internal Revenue Service, that's untaxed liquor.

For years, my uncle, Louis, was the number one 'shine still operator in the mountains, and he and Dad made a lot of illegal liquor and sold it. Evidently, they made a good amount of money, as my father had one of the fastest Model 'T' cars in existence, one of the few automobiles in the Saluda Mountains.

No, Dad wasn't famous like Junior Johnson and some of the other boys. He didn't get into racing. But he did have a record. Yup, a prison record, for transporting booze.

Louis and Dad had the reputation of making the best moonshine booze in the hills. The Sheriff of Polk County, the local Judge and the head of the State Police were frequent customers, as were the Mayors and chiefs of police of several of the nearby towns.

I understand that when Louis would pour a little of his liquor into a saucer and set fire to it, it would burn a beautiful blue flame similar to natural gas. That's supposed to prove that it was pure.

Anyway, the local Gestapo, also known as 'the Revenue Boys' (Actually that branch of the Department of the Treasury eventually became the Alcohol, Tobacco and Firearms) needed to maintain a certain arrest quota in order to keep the people from Washington from investigating. Every year or so, one person or another would "be caught" and would plead guilty. As a rule, the fine would be $500.00 and probation for one year. The Revenue Boys would make sure that no one violated their probation by being

181

caught again during that one year. The government agents knew everyone who was involved with making 'shine and would only arrest one per year.

This time, I suppose it was my father's turn. Louis and some of the others were supposed to appear in court and pay the fine, but a strange Judge was assigned to the Tryon courthouse, and he sentenced my father to a two-year jail sentence. And the Judge confiscated my father's automobile. That wasn't according to the 'rules'. But, it was too late for anyone to do anything.

~*~

All of we kids walked softly when Dad was around. That wasn't too often, as Dad would walk 20 miles to work in construction every morning (for the princely sum of fifty-cents per day – this was during World War II) and 20 miles back home, until he could finally afford another Model 'T' automobile.

Dad presented a scary, authoritative image, but I can't remember him ever punishing any of the kids. He certainly had the physique, after years of carrying two bags of sugar, one on each shoulder and each weighing 100 pounds, for miles across the mountain to the concealed moonshine still located deep in the mountains near Chimney Rock, North Carolina. Seems like the cold, pure mountain water that fed from natural springs was just what Louis needed to put the final kick in his potent but untaxed liquor.

Our situation when I was a kid was one of abject poverty. That hadn't always been the situation for our family, according to my parents and neighbors. Actually, during the early 1920's, my father was reasonably affluent for the time, earning goodly sums of money transporting and selling illegal alcohol.

182

Being frugal, a character trait that lasted until his death, Dad saved most of his money and, trusting his government, Dad had his money in a bank account with the Bank of Rutherford County, in Rutherfordton, North Carolina. And then catastrophe – referred to as the 'Great Depression' – struck.

We lived some fifteen miles west of Rutherfordton in the foothills of the mountains. Dad had purchased a little more than fifty acres of timberland and negotiated with a neighbor to acquire an additional fifty acres. He had agreed to the purchase price of $10.00 per acre and had promised the landowner that he would pay for the land on that day.

Dad traveled into Rutherfordton to withdraw five hundred dollars from his bank account. As he arrived at the bank, he saw that there were several men standing on the wood sidewalk in front of the bank, each man holding a sub-machine gun.

Do you remember the old 'chopper' submachine guns from the Elliot Ness "The Untouchables" television series? Well, that's the kind of automatic guns that the Treasury Department issued to its agents during that period.

A military truck was backed up to the front door of the bank and men were carrying bags out of the bank and placing them in the truck.

Inquiries led to the information that these were U.S. Treasury agents and Revenue agents. The government agents were removing all of the money from the bank. The United States Government was confiscating all of the money. Every single, solitary dollar. Including the dollars that my father had believed belonged to him.

Guess what? The money was never returned.

Dad hated the Treasury Department. He really hated the 'tax people', as he called them, with a passion.

183

Not just because the Treasury Department had been instrumental in him receiving a two-year prison sentence. But now they had taken all of his money.

From the date the 'tax people' took his money, Dad had no liking for any part of the Federal Government and an especial anger toward the Treasury Department. Can you blame him? He railed for much of the rest of his life against "those gol-durn revenuers" and "them tax bastards." "May they rot in Hell!" His hatred was white-hot. Do you blame him?

And I'm named "Junior."

~*~

By working hard as a carpenter, Dad was able to save a few dollars here and there. I can remember him and my mother, by the light of a kerosene lamp, counting the hard-earned money he had been able to save. It seemed so little, but I guess at the time it was a lot. Eventually, he had the five hundred dollars to pay the man who had deeded the fifty acres to my father. The man had trusted Dad and was willing to wait for his money. Dad never broke a promise. Not to anyone; not for any reason.

~*~

Those fifty acres of land became an important part of my life at the time I was starting the eighth grade in our elementary school. At the time, grade one through eight went to the Sunnyview Elementary

184

School and grades nine through twelve attended the Mill Springs High School.

The land that Dad had bought was heavily wooded. Dad sold some of the timber—the larger of the trees—to help pay for the land. He allowed my brother and I to cut pulpwood in order to earn money.

My brother is two and one-half years older than I. Running and playing in the hilly terrain gave both of us a certain amount of strength, but we were by no means anywhere near as strong as the man who helped us. He was a big, strong black man, the largest that I had ever seen.

A quick explanation is in order. Living in the countryside as we did, our neighbor on one side was a poor, white family that was even more destitute than my own. On the other side, lived several black families. All of the kids, black and white, boy and girl, played together and didn't think about race. With the adults, it was different.

The men would work together in the fields and in making molasses out of the sugar cane when it was harvested. When mealtime came, the white men sat down to eat along with the head of the black family. The other black men and the women waited. The kids ate last, black and white together. I guess no one thought that the black kids would contaminate the white kids. Wish the adults on both sides could realize that.

Charlie, the person who was helping my brother and me, owned a big truck. It was agreed that my brother and I would cut the pulpwood and load it on the truck. Charlie would then haul the pulpwood to Rutherfordton and we would share the money we received.

Pulpwood, at the time, was approximately six inches in diameter and four feet long. And heavy.

185

A cord of pulpwood was four feet high, four feet wide and eight feet long. Charlie's truck would haul twelve cords at one time, and it was my brother and I who were required to cut the wood and load it on the truck. Then, we were allowed to ride with Charlie to Rutherfordton, where we would offload the pulpwood onto the flatbed of a railroad car. Without Charlie's help, I don't think we could have made it.

Pulpwood sold in Rutherfordton for sixteen dollars per cord. Charlie's share for helping cut, load and haul was one-half, or eight dollars. Dad took one-half as owner of the property. That left four dollars for my brother and I to share.

I was rich.

Want to guess what I bought with my part? I bought a pair of pants.

~*~

It was exactly fifteen miles from our home to Rutherfordton. Transportation was not easily available. Even at ten to twelve cents per gallon, gasoline was expensive. Most families living in bucolic areas received mail-order catalogues from Sears, Roebuck and Company and from Montgomery Ward. It was in this venue, gazing at pictures of desired items in awe, that most rural families did their shopping.

Just as in most poor families, the younger son wears hand-me-downs, and I was no exception. But this day, things were different. I had enough money to order my very first *new* pair of pants, and I chose carefully. Red. I wanted something red. Really, really red. I mean, fire engine red. Wow! Boy, would I be something.

186

It seemed to take forever, but finally those pants arrived. I was eager for the first day of school. When the time finally arrived, I excitedly climbed into the bus and traveled to school

It was on that day that I had my first—and—only fight in school. Franklin, the school bully, began to make fun of my new pants and I punched him right in the mouth. Caused his nose to bleed. The blood that flowed from his nose was almost as bright red as the brilliant red pants that I had bought with my share of the pulpwood money.

I never wore those pants again, and for most of my life, I have hated the color of red.

Another first occurred that day. My first spanking in school Yes, folks, there really was a time in the past when the principal of a school could discipline a rowdy child without being sued by mal-directed parents intent on getting rich at the expense of someone else.

~*~

Life in the mountains was simple. Simple and hard. Everyone had to work just to make ends meet.

Dad worked as a carpenter and Mom worked in the textile mill in Rutherfordton. She would often work the midnight shift, which required her to have a car. She would come home exhausted and need to rest, so the kids stayed out of her way, enjoying the freedom that children have when their parents are away or asleep.

Part of that freedom was learning to smoke. I believe that every child looks at his parents for guidance. The parents, often without realizing it, serve as a role model. Both Mom and Dad smoked. Dad's

187

brand was Camel and Mom smoked Salem brand menthol cigarettes.

Wanting to be like Dad, I would steal some of his cigarettes and sneak away to smoke. Of course, I only smoked in front of one of the little girls that I was trying to impress. I don't remember that I made much of an impression, but I do know that for the next thirty-five years, I contributed my share of cigarette taxes to the Treasury Department.

Yep, I was hooked.

~*~

Mom working at the textile mill led to changes in our life. The only good thing I remember about Mom's work was that at Christmas time each year, the mill would give her two bags of 'goodies'; oranges, apples, nuts and candy. Most of the time that was our only Christmas.

Another pleasant memory about the mill was that the management would allow a blind man to stand just outside the exit gate on each payday. The blind man would play his guitar and place his hat on the ground at his feet. Most of the workers would donate some of their money to help the blind man.

Just as an aside, it turned out that the blind man was one of the richest men in the county. In fact, he had the first television set in his home that any person in the entire county owned. His son was one of the very few who drove a car to school.

Looking back, life did indeed seem simple at the time, but my heart was about to be broken for the second time. I would lose my second girlfriend. This time, I was the one who had to move away.

~*~

Mom's work was taking a toll on her and she needed to move closer to her work. That decision was made easier by the disastrous results of our trying to dig a well.

Our house was sitting on the top of a ridge, sort of like a good-sized hill. Our water source was a spring located some 500 yards down one side. There, my sisters and my grandmother had put a huge black pot that was used to boil our clothes. (That's the way people used to wash their clothes at the time) The water was pure and sweet, but it was a pain to carry the water up the hill every day. Both Mom and Dad wanted running water in our house but lacked a nearby source. Dad decided that we would dig a well.

We started. I seem to remember that the well was about six feet in diameter, and Dad, my brother and I would get into the hole and dig, lifting the dirt out using a bucket and a winch. We would hit rock from time to time, and Dad would use dynamite to break up the stones so we could remove them from the well. After a long time, Dad had enough. We had dug out about 25 to 30 feet of soil. We stopped. (Years later, Dad moved back to the same location. He had a professional company drill a well for him. They struck water at 875 feet. Good thing he gave up or we'd still be digging.)

We moved into a house in a small town, Spindale, North Carolina. Without the necessity of having to do a lot of farm work, spare time was plentiful. Being a quick study in school, I found that I had more spare time than I had ever had.

Part of that time was spent working in a movie theater. Mom signed my papers when I was only 12, certifying that I was 14 so that I could be employed. At the same time, I became a rather good bowler and a pool (billiards) hustler. Made more money bowling and shooting pool than I made working at the theater.

That move also brought me into my first contact with the law.

Nothing major. Some of the town's teens and I would often hang out together. There was a church under construction at the time. I seem to remember that it was the First Baptist Church of Spindale. The 3-story steel skeleton was erected and that was a better attraction than Disney World.

At night, the workmen would go home and the kids would come out. We would climb the steel beams and walk on the narrow girders high above the ground. At night. Of course, none of us ever believed that we would get hurt. Nor did we.

However, one night a neighbor saw us kids playing and called the cops. The sheriff and his deputy (the only deputy) came with their siren screaming and caught a couple of the other kids. I descended the rear girder headfirst, reached the ground safely and made my getaway. Safe. Or so I thought.

The following day, the deputy sheriff came to the theater where I was working. (If I had completed my schoolwork, I was allowed to leave school at 1:00 p.m. in order to work) He told me that the sheriff wanted to see me. You had better believe that I was scared stiff.

The sheriff told me that although he didn't catch me, my companions had told him that I was on the church with them. He just warned me that if I should repeat the action, he would see my parents. That scared me even worse.

I had been raised to believe that you never told on someone else, and this was my first experience at

190

being "ratted out." Alas. Had I only paid attention to that lesson.

    I didn't.

    Damn.

~*~

    Sorry to get so far off the subject, but old memories just keep popping up.

    As you may surmise, Dad's relationships with the federal government had not served him well. He felt betrayed by his own leaders. Did Dad pass that hatred along to us kids? I don't really think so, as my siblings have had no difficulty with the Internal Revenue Service. And, I'm not sure that it played any large part in my actions, although, just like my father, I have very little respect for any agency that enforces such a punitive tax system.

    However, I would be lying if I didn't admit that the government's actions against my father had some effect on me. After all, I have my father's name.

    Oh, and there is one other small, tiny thing. I don't like the Internal Revenue Service. Not even one small, itty-bitty bit. Not any at all. I've heard too many true stories about their actions.

~*~

    How about you? Are you really, truly fond of the Internal Revenue Service? Look me straight in the eye and don't lie. Do you enjoy paying taxes on money that you worked for, that you earned; taxes that are spent in ways that you do not approve? Taxes that are collected to support organizations and foreign nations that you do not like? Taxes that go to benefit those who are not paying their fair share of taxes?

Sure you do.

Not.

No? Do you know anyone who does?

Well, neither do I.

That being said, my personal feelings as to the Internal Revenue Service really played no major part in my decision vis-à-vis the IRS or in my decision to let William write my story.

In fact, my personal feelings inclined me to tell William not only no, but Hell No! Not because I haven't led an interesting life, it has been a blast. And not because I believe this book won't sell. Actually, I'm quite sure it will.

A nightmare that I have is the book will actually become a run-away best seller, and that I will make a lot of money.

Guess who will be there with their hand stuck out? Right. The IRS.

It galls me that they will get a major share of any income this book generates, and they didn't participate in its writing.

But, on the other hand, wait a minute! The IRS did indeed participate. Without their actions, there would be no story to tell. So, I guess you could say that the IRS is my partner in writing this book. An unwilling and unwelcome partner I agree, but a partner, nonetheless. I suppose that I should extend my thanks to the IRS, but somehow I just can't.

~*~

Before you ask, there's really nothing funny or amusing or even honorable about being labeled an 'IRS Cheat." Although William and I have tried to inject a little humor in a morose subject, the laughter stops when the IRS stands up. I'm just trying to keep the tears from starting.

As I've already said, it wasn't my goal or intent to become an IRS cheat. It just kind of happened almost as an accident, starting with a small false entry and growing from there.

And I didn't intend to make a full-time career of it although I certainly didn't resist the temptation.

Oh, sure! I can almost hear your thinking. Here's just another rip-off, a promise to tell the facts and this person is going to give a bunch of alibis and excuses.

To that, I say: Nay! No! Nix! If you keep reading, you will learn all that you want to know about me. In fact, you may well learn much more than you really want to know.

~*~

During my early years of learning about the income tax software and the Internal Revenue Code, the small modifications that I helped my friends and clients make didn't seem all that serious. In fact, during the early part of the '90's it was almost as if it were a game; us against the IRS.

Working with Sanjiv—Andy—it was easy to pick up on his attitude that what we were doing, at least at first, what we were doing was to help the lower-income tax-filers get a little larger slice of the pie. Especially helping those who were single mothers of the minority races. As Bill, Jr. (my son) says, we actually

193

thought that we were helping people who needed it. At least, it did at first. After all, it didn't seem that the money we were giving away would hurt anyone. Anyway, the Government could afford it. And it was just a small bit of revenge.

Further, neither Andy, my son or I—nor any of the preparers—did what we did just for the money, with the possible exception of William P. For William P., it seemed that it was always the money, which he needed to pay for the copious amounts of expensive Scotch whisky that he drank and to support the many young exotic dancers that always seemed to be hanging around him.

In fact, the fees that we charged our clients were less than the fees charged by either H & R Block or by Jackson-Hewitt tax preparation offices. Andy had previously owned a Jackson-Hewitt franchise and had opened other offices in Kannapolis, where he had obtained an option on a second franchise, being unable to pay the full twenty-five thousand dollars per franchise at that time.

A Jackson-Hewitt franchise covered the residents of one zip code exclusively, but could draw from surrounding areas without penalty. Unfortunately, Andy only held an option on the area including Kannapolis. His opening an office in that location violated his franchise agreement. He wasn't supposed to operate a Jackson-Hewitt in the area until the second half of the purchase price was paid.

As a result, in early 1994, Andy lost his Jackson-Hewitt designation. This caused a lot of problems, as the Jackson-Hewitt owned the Electronic Filing authorization number. Effectively, this put Andy out of business, but he scrambled around and found another tax preparation firm that used the same tax preparation software that Andy was using. The owner

194

of that company, Lawrence, about whom you will hear a lot more shortly, agreed to serve as a transmitter until Andy could obtain another Electronic Filing authorization number.

It was a matter of only a few days, and Andy was back in operation, determined to build his business bigger than ever. Between his desire to make sure that his clients received the maximum refund and his intent to grow, all deductions and all dependents were allowed to pass unchallenged. And I enthusiastically joined in, as did many of the preparers who worked with Andy. Business grew rapidly until the bank indicator fiasco in 1994-1995.

~*~

With the changes in the dependant filing status and the slower refunds of the Earned Income Tax Credit affecting our business, focus shifted to the self-employed individuals and the small businessman or businesswoman.

I referred earlier to Amway. Actually, it could have been any multi-level marketing plan except that I enjoyed the Amway vitamins, and Amway had more products. I found it wasn't necessary to be a fanatic about the Company, simply buy enough products (mine were vitamins) to qualify for the minimum and recruit others to do the same. By qualifying for the minimum, I would be entitled to a small rebate check.

In actuality, one became a distributor of the Amway products, much as retail stores became distributors of furniture, clothing and other merchandise. And the more members that one recruited, and the more products that were purchased,

195

used or sold by the group, the larger the rebate check to the person who had recruited the members.

I thought I saw a great light and a brilliant idea. It seemed a natural to recruit my tax clients.

To recruit members, or a 'down-line' as it was known, often required repeated trips to different places to meet with people and to expose them to the Amway system. These trips, including lodging, meals, etc., were, of course, deductible as business expenses.

Suddenly, I had a 'brilliant' idea. I thought that I would have the best of all worlds. People would join Amway under me, do the minimum and qualify for a small check. We would prepare their income tax returns, including the Schedule 'C' for the small business, writing off all of the deductions that the tax-filer could suggest, whether actually incurred or not. The tax-filer would enjoy the larger refund, Andy would enjoy the increased business and I would move up in Amway, earning larger residual checks.

Originally, I had tried to recruit the Earned Income Tax Credit clients, believing that this group would work hard because they needed additional income. But I found out, after a year or so, that the mentality of clients in this income bracket was not that of a business owner. I also found out that poverty is also a mental state and people are not inclined to change their mental status. In fact, the deductions for business expenses served little purpose with a person on limited income. Additionally, that type of a person didn't want to spend $160.00 per month in expectation of a larger refund and a rebate later down the road. Still, the program should have worked, as the $160.00 would be spent acquiring products such as soap, detergents, cosmetics, etc, that the person would be buying from a retail store.

196

Those negative results led to my shifting sights toward those earning more money, people who could benefit from a business that incurred a loss. Surely, these individuals could be motivated by both the promise of additional income and substantial deductions so that they would pay fewer taxes.

The theory worked very well, but the practice didn't fulfill its promise. Many did join Amway, and used the system's intent to minimize their tax bills. Business expenses, many of which must have occurred only in the client's mind, were used as deductions for clients whose income was over $80,000. These clients were able to reduce taxable income to astonishingly low amounts. In fact, more than a few were able to claim a refund check for the Earned Income Tax Credit simply because the 'business expenses' claimed for belonging to Amway lowered their adjusted gross income below the disqualifying threshold.

Still, a few did join and try, in some small way, to follow the Amway system.

In fact, one client joined for the sole purpose of using the Amway system to justify the many trips he took to exotic places, including the Bahamas. He also did the minimum by buying some $180.00 worth of vitamins with the stipulation that instead of sending the vitamins to his home, I should have them delivered to the Salvation Army's Soup Kitchen. He asked that I obtain a receipt. Turns out that he used the Amway distributorship to deduct thousands in expenses and then wrote off the $180.00 per month as a charitable contribution since the vitamins were given to an approved charitable organization.

Sort of like double dipping, isn't it?

Another client, a Mexican, became an Amway distributor. He and his wife and two children traveled to Matazalan, Mexico to recruit his father and mother.

197

His tax return for that year was audited by the IRS, and the auditor permitted the expenses for the two adults, co-owners of the business, which included the price of two airline tickets and lodging at one of the better hotels for 5 nights as well as food and meals. The auditor disallowed any expenses claimed for the children because the tax-filer had forgotten to appoint them as directors of the business, a matter corrected before the next trip. The auditor did allow the cost of one round of golf at the local country club. The tax-filer's father and mother did become distributors of Amway, which is an international organization. Of the $7,560 that he spent, he was allowed to deduct $6,450 as business expenses, which resulted in a tax savings of nearly $3,000.

Afterwards, as the mother and father were distributors the tax-filer's "down-line," it became necessary for the tax-filer to make regular trips to Mexico to assist his down-line members solicit other members.

Before I lost contact, I understand that the Mexican down-line is doing quite well and is continuing to grow. Part of that may be that because the residents in Mexico belong to the tax-filer's down-line, the United States Embassy will issue a business visa, permitting the Mexican resident to visit the United States to consult with his "up-line"(a legal way to enter the U.S.).

As a matter of information, I have family in Europe. Both my wife, who is from France, and I enjoy traveling to Europe and have established a down-line business that is composed of several people, not all of whom are family. We find that the efforts to recruit distributors there allow us to deduct the expense of international travel.

198

Most people who joined Amway, however, were looking for instant results, and that just doesn't happen. Few, if any, of those who joined under me continued to do the minimum required. They would use the system only for the purpose of reducing their tax bill, and that didn't put any money in my pocket. Eventually, I dropped the idea.

Still, completing the income tax returns and helping people remember that, to their surprise, they really did own a business, was a bonus for them although their business never made a profit.

The IRS rule was that a business had to "show a profit motive three of the first five years of business." Showing a profit motive, in my opinion didn't mean that the business had to prosper, only that it was trying to move from a loss to a profit.

And there were many takers.

Naturally, all of the tax-filers enjoyed the benefits of the deductions and, of course, they would keep proper records.

Ha!

And, naturally, all of them would provide those records to the Internal Revenue Service in the event of an audit in order to justify the deductions. Right?

Not!

The only thing that melts faster than a tax-filer that knows he or she has crossed the line and has to undergo an IRS audit is an ice cube in the middle of the Sahara Desert in the midst of a heat wave. And even that would be a virtual dead heat.

~*~

The first of my 'Amway' clients that I discovered being audited was a man named after the second most famous person in the movie, "Gone With The Wind." You know the one I mean, the one that said, "Damn" to Charlotte.

I would have expected the client to contact me and would have attended the audit in his place, which was allowed, but there was no contact made and the client attended the audit alone.

The report that I received later from IRS investigators said that this tax-filer claimed that he had no business venture and that he knew nothing about any of the business expenses that were used as deductions and that were listed on the tax return, and that the tax preparer, Bill Jackson (me) must have made them up.

I made them up? By myself? And he didn't know anything about them?

Guess who got the money? One hint, t'weren't yours truly.

Duh!

As an aside, and as you will learn more about later, I had the occasion to retain the now-retired head of the Internal Revenue Service in the Forsyth-Guilford County area as an expert witness. He informed me that in virtually every case, more than twenty thousand during his career, that not one tax-filer had ever admitted knowing that false information had been included on the income tax return. Not one, in over twenty years and over 20,000 cases of fraudulent returns. Doesn't that just ring your bell?

Now, back to the situation on hand. I had learned that another of my personal clients was scheduled for audit. I contacted him and asked to attend the audit with him and his wife. Both of them agreed.

200

The client worked for a security firm and had a side business. The side business was cleaning floors for one of the pizza chain stores. The client cleaned approximately nine of the stores, on a rotating basis.

As the client worked from his business office that he maintained in his home, the Internal Revenue Code allows the deduction of mileage from his home to the restaurant and back to the home. There were other deductions for supplies and other materials used. The work was done under written contract between the client and the pizza chain.

During the preparation of the income tax return, I questioned the client about the distances from his home to each location. Then I calculated the mileage based on those distances and took the proper deduction.

In addition, the tax-filer's wife worked two jobs. She would leave home and go to one job. Then she would leave that job and drive to the second job. Afterwards, she would return to the first jobsite. Finally, after work was complete, she would return home.

The Internal Revenue Code does not permit deductions for the mileage from home to the first place of employment, but does permit deduction for the mileage from jobsite number one to jobsite number two and return. That mileage was calculated and entered into the joint return.

At the time of the audit, the wife was in the late stages of pregnancy and was scared. The tax-filer was also frightened, as the Internal Revenue Service Auditor and her supervisor were both in the room. When questioned about the mileage, the tax-filer denied any knowledge of how the mileage was computed.

At that point, I interrupted. I stated that I was the "paid preparer" who had prepared the return, that I had filed a Form 2848, a Taxpayer's Power of Attorney, and as such I had the right to speak on behalf of the tax-filer. With the consent of the auditor, I asked the client if he could remember my coming to his home before the tax return was filed. He stated that he did. I asked if he remembered riding in my car from his house to each of the restaurants, calculating the round-trip mileage and returning to his house. He stated that he did. I asked if he remembered reading the dates from his day calendar as to which dates he cleaned each restaurant. He stated that he did. I asked if he remembered sitting with me in my office and helping me calculate the total mileage. He stated that he did.

The auditor's supervisor interrupted at that point and asked the client if he had brought his day journal with him to the audit. He stated that he hadn't remembered to bring it. The audit was dismissed upon the condition that he would provide the auditor a copy of the journal.

Why tell you all of this? To help you understand the pressure that the tax-filer faces when he or she comes face to face with the Internal Revenue Service Dragon.

Just like I said, an ice cube in the Sahara Desert. In the midst of a heat spell. On a hot, sun-filled day. In the middle of August.

~*~

So, what happened with the first client? Old Mister 'Gone With The Wind' himself melted. He not only told the Internal Revenue Service that he had no

202

idea where the deductions came from but that they were completely false, that he had never owned a business (despite the fact that he was an Amway distributor, which is an independent business) and that the tax preparer (me) must have made up the entire thing. He was willing to testify to that in court, if required.

If that wasn't bad enough, four of his friends also agreed to testify that I had provided them with the same type false information and had personally prepared their income tax returns. Only one small lie. A woman working in William P.'s office, an area that I always avoided during income tax filing season, had prepared two of the returns. A woman working in Andy's office prepared the remaining two, but I must admit that I did provide her with the deductions that the 'Gone With The Wind' client and I had agreed upon.

Wasn't aware? Didn't know? My back end! He knew every number and was trying to add even more, but I always tried to encourage a client to limit his or her claims in order to avoid red flags that causes audits.

Adding insult to injury, the following year (before the IRS audit) the same client came to our office. I was away and my son was working there. He prepared the tax return for the client, using the information that had remained in the computer from the prior year's return. The client provided the changes in deductions and all information in order that the return could be prepared. At the audit, which occurred later, he swore that he did not provide any information and that the tax preparer must have put down false information that the client didn't authorize.

Just a bit of information: all tax-filers must sign a document either for electronic filing or on the 1040 mail-in return which says, in brief, that the taxpayer has

203

reviewed the tax return and certifies, *under penalty of perjury, that the information contained therein is "true, accurate and complete."*

Duh!

Even so, the Internal Revenue Service is not interested in prosecuting some small-time tax-filer who swindles the United States out of a few thousand dollars. The reaction is to force repayment, perhaps with a penalty and interest. On the other hand, the Internal Revenue Service is ready, willing and able—even eager—to prosecute any tax preparer who prepares a tax return for anyone that contains false information. Or, even someone who just gives a person advice on how to submit false information on his or her tax return. Even a friend.

~*~

Federal warrants were issued for my son and I. Turns out that Lawrence, who had become my partner in 1995, had informed the Internal Revenue Service that he suspected that William P. and I were doing false tax returns. Lawrence was the details person of the partnership and I was the marketing end. Lawrence was scared of William P. who was under covert investigation by the IRS at the time. Seems like one of his clients resented him for taking too much of the refund and had informed the IRS.

Lawrence had suggested—even ordered— that I avoid William P., but had not given me a reason. In as much as William P. was providing us with more than four hundred tax returns per year, I didn't see any reason to shun the man, but it later became apparent that Lawrence was afraid that he might be tainted by William P.'s actions.

Despite the thousands of tax returns that my son and I had generated and filed, the IRS could only find five people that the agency could coerce into stating that either my son or I had helped file false returns. And all five of them were close friends of one another.

The charges against me were preparing and filing five false income tax returns and conspiracy to defraud the United States of America. The charges against my son were five charges of filing a false income tax return and conspiracy to defraud the United States of America.

~*~

Conspiracy.

Watch out for that one.

The government's "Weapons of Mass Destruction."

The United States government and all prosecuting attorneys has found this word to be a great weapon and it is relatively simple to prosecute an individual on a conspiracy charge. Without getting too deep into details or debating the fine points of law, let me just comment. There is no way to disprove the charge.

And, in the case of my son and me, there was an additional reason to file the conspiracy charge. The fact was that the same individual was willing to swear that he provided no false information and that the two of us had fabricated both of the returns. This, despite the evidence that only the tax-filer had benefited from the transaction and that the tax-filer had signed a document stating that he had examined the tax returns,

205

that the returns were true, accurate and complete, and that he, the tax-filer, under penalty of perjury, had provided the information to the tax preparer.

Duh.

In my case, I had indeed worked with the tax-filer, knowing full well that most, if not all, of the information regarding the business was bogus; that the tax-filer and I had jointly developed the numbers and submitted them to one of the other tax preparers to complete the return.

In the case of my son, the information was provided by the tax-filer on a sheet of paper stating what was the amount of each business expense. Using the information that was in the computer from the prior year, my son simply completed the tax return, assuming that the tax-filer was providing legitimate and accurate information. I did what I did knowingly, my son felt that he had prepared a legal return.

The primary reason that the government uses the 'conspiracy' charge is that it adds an extra charge to any crime and it may enhance the sentence that the Judge gives a guilty party. That's a pretty big hammer.

This creates a lot of pressure on a person charged with a crime and with conspiracy to try to negotiate a plea. Losing a case involving either charge may well result in a long-term prison sentence.

In our particular situation, the prosecution had one additional leverage point. And it was a strong one.

Because of our family situation—a physically handicapped family member who didn't drive and was unable to work—there was an urgent need that both my son and I not be absent at the same time. If we were tried and found guilty, it was likely that we would both be sentenced to prison. That would create a great hardship on family members who depended on us for livelihood and transportation.

Two court-appointed attorneys—one for me and one for my son— consulted with us and with the U.S. Prosecuting Attorney. Both of our lawyers agreed that should either of us be found guilty, the likelihood of the conviction of the second person under the conspiracy charge was similar to a professional football team kicking an extra point. It was virtually a given. Under those circumstances, both of us would be sentenced to active time in a federal prison.

With that incentive, it became an urgent necessity to negotiate a deal with the legal authorities that would allow either my son or I to avoid incarceration, and that's the way it came down.

We decided that, since I had the more severe charges, I would plead guilty and accept a sentence without appeal. My son would receive a house-arrest sentence and probation that would not require him to be away from home.

I was given a sentence similar to the 'Martha Stewart' sentence; that is, five months in a federal prison camp and five months at home with an electronic monitor.

The sentence that I received was at the low end of the sentence guidelines. Although the Judge didn't say so, I believe that he gave the lightest sentence that he could give because he was able to determine that neither my son nor I received any monetary benefits from the erroneous filings. In fact, I feel certain that I may not have been sentenced to prison at all, except that the IRS wanted to make an example out of me. When I had been asked by the IRS investigator why I had accepted my clients' deductions without question and had not made my clients prove their deductions to me, I told her that I was not working for the IRS, I was working on behalf of the client.

207

After she told me that it was my responsibility
to determine the validity of each deduction, I made a
bad mistake. I told her to go and perform a physically
impossible task on herself. Guess I must have made her
mad. And she got even.

As a personal note, try to stay away from
prisons. Even the federal correctional facility at Butner,
North Carolina isn't that pleasant. Nor are the people
that you meet. In fact, they're mostly a bunch of
criminals. And I'm not just talking about the convicts.

~*~

Released again into society, I met Kyle, whom I
have already mentioned. Kyle was from East Texas and
was the father of a young man who worked with my
son in a construction company. I was also helping my
son, and Kyle came along with his son every day, as his
driver.

Kyle was near my age – in fact, two years older
– and like me, felt himself a little too old to be carrying
lumber or driving nails. We were each looking for a
situation that wasn't so physically demanding.

Kyle had lived near Mexicans as a child, and as
such was somewhat literate with the Spanish language.
Not fluent by any means, but sufficient to be able to
converse in small talk. He was not familiar with income
tax preparation or the computer software that was in
use, but it didn't take long for him to learn the 'ropes',
as he would say.

Lacking the funds to rent office space, although
I still had a number of computers on hand that I had
inherited when Andy moved to California with his
parents, I began to approach Mexican and Hispanic

stores, with the idea of appearing in the store one or two days per week and preparing income tax returns for the customers of the store. With the generous help of the storeowners, most of whom were either tax clients or bookkeeping clients or both, the business began to increase to the point that Kyle and I were able to open a tax preparation office in Winston Salem.

With my record, I would not qualify for approval as an Electronic Filer (EF) with the Internal Revenue Service, but Kyle did. With the EF number, we were able to generate Refund Anticipation Loans and do electronic filing, which caused the business to continue to grow.

By this time, I was certain that I would never make a lot of money pounding on keyboards, so I moved from the tax office, leaving it in the hands of Kyle, who brought his daughter-in-law into the business. This allowed Kyle to open another office in High Point, with the concept of multiple offices concentrating primarily on lower-income people and Hispanics.

Using the increased income from these offices, I was able to move into an area that had really captured my attention and drew me away from income tax preparation. Working with business owners to develop offshore ventures.

~*~

You can meet the most interesting people when you are in prison.

David, a young man from Kentucky, was serving a sentence at the same time that I was a guest

209

of the United States Bureau of Prisons. He had been found guilty of arson and fraud. Turns out that he was convicted of burning down his own house and collecting the insurance, some one hundred and eighty thousand dollars.

David swears that he didn't 'torch' the house, although his girlfriend testified that he had left several expensive guns, a Rolex watch, and a mink coat at her house two days before the house burned. She became angry with David and called the police.

There's an old saying, "Hell hath no fury like a woman scorned." If it wouldn't make me seem to be a woman-hater, I would say that it seems to be true. But then, David wasn't the nicest of people.

David had a situation. He and his family were farmers in Kentucky and had been for a number of years. His father had reached the age of eighty and under the advise of a local attorney had split his property, almost one thousand acres of highly productive farm land, giving roughly one-half to David and one-half to his brother, Charles.

Complicating the situation was that at a later time the IRS had performed an audit on the family. In fact, the IRS had audited every farmer in the entire county. Almost every one of the farmers had been using the same accounting firm, an accountant named Steve.

Steve had been preparing the returns and then suddenly decided to resign from the firm and go into sales, or some other line of work.

It just so happened that the audits began less than three months after Steve had resigned.

Guess what?

Every farmer had been taking deductions for equipment, fertilizer, seeds, etc. for a number of years. And, again, guess what?

210

Not a single farmer had the receipts needed to prove that he or she had spent the money listed on the tax return.

The IRS rule is: no receipt, no deduction.

Final result of the audits for David and his family was that for the years 1992 through 1995, Daddy owed $75,000.00; Charles owed $143,000.00; and David owed $115,000.00. In addition, there was a grandson who owed $26,000.00. The total sum owed by the family was over $359,999.00.

The IRS likes to get paid. In fact, the IRS insists on getting paid. On several occasions, in that same county, the IRS had seized homes and farms, and David was afraid that the IRS would grab his land and that of his family.

Another fear was that the courts would require that David sell his land to repay the insurance company for the money he had obtained by fraud. The total of all the debt, insurance and IRS tax combined, was over $500,000.00.

David had one additional thing that he read every night in his cell. A travel book about a country named Belize.

~*~

A trip to Kentucky to meet with Charles was vital. In the Holiday Inn Downtown, located on West Broadway in Louisville, a meeting took place that was to change the direction of all my efforts. At the meeting, Charles and I discussed the ramifications and the potential difficulties that lay ahead. If the IRS didn't grab the land, then the insurance company would; at least, that portion that belonged to David.

The land was quite important to the farming operations of the family. Holding quotas in burley tobacco, the family needed all of the land in order to plant the tobacco for which they held quotas. If the insurance company took one-half, the family's income would be drastically reduced. And, of course, if the IRS confiscated all the land, the entire family would be homeless.

It appeared that with David serving a prison sentence, we had a little time to take action. The first action would be to protect David's land against the insurance company as I suspected the insurance company would have less patience than the IRS.

A corporation was quickly formed.

An attorney drew up a 'quit-claim' deed conveying David's land to the Corporation. Charles took the deed to the prison, where his brother signed the deed. A notary – well paid – notarized the document, which was then recorded. The deed had been backdated to before David had been sentenced to prison.

At the same time, Charles signed a deed conveying the balance of the land to the same corporation. The corporation executed contracts with the tobacco buyers in Harlan for the harvest of the farm.

This allowed several events to take place.

~*~

David was released from prison and was employed at $6.25 per hour with a company that I created. Part of David's sentence had been to reimburse the insurance company for the amount of

money that he had received. He was to repay the
insurance company at the rate of sixty thousand dollars
per year. He didn't have the money, and his brother
and father both didn't want to pay the money if there
was a way out.

Using a local Louisville attorney, we petitioned
the Court on David's behalf. During a hearing with the
Federal Judge, it was proposed that David make
payments in line with his employment. After much
discussion, and 'cussing from the insurance attorneys,
the Judge ruled that David was virtually a pauper, that
whoever had set up the plan was very sharp and that
there was nothing the Court could do about it. The
Judge stated that he simply didn't believe that David
was smart enough to have developed such a plan, and
that he – the judge – was very suspicious of David's
brother. However, the Court had no access to the
brother. The judge's ruling was that David would pay
$400.00 per month until the $180,000 was paid.

David had been sentenced to a period of two
years on probation. During those two years David
made his payment promptly on the first of each month.
As the payments started on the fourth month of his
probation, David had to make 21 payments of $400.00
each month, or a total of $8,400.00. Once probation
was up, David ceased to be employed by the company
that I had set up and began working for his own
corporation, which was an offshore company that I will
describe a little later.

He never paid another dime.

~*~

Daddy had no land and no assets, simply a
lifetime estate in his home, which had been included in

213

the land that he gave to his sons. As he had zero assets, there was nothing for the IRS to attach. At his age, it is unlikely that he will ever have assets and should he acquire them, it would be in the name of his offshore company.

~*~

Charles became an employee of the same company that hired David. Charles's job is to operate the corporation that owns the land and to serve as general manager. For this, he is paid a salary. The salary is relatively small but is still sufficient to generate a tax refund from the IRS. This refund is in the area of $500 to $700 each year. Of course, the IRS seizes that refund to apply to the debt that Charles owes. Charles also has zero assets so there is no property for the IRS to attach.

Charles has made an offer in compromise of some $3,000.00 in order to settle his debt, but the IRS has refused to consider it. Meanwhile, Charles doesn't worry too much about that when he is spending his vacation in a condo in Florida that the corporation owns. Of course, the income flows into the corporation, and the profits, if any, are reflected on the corporate tax return.

Right.

If.

~*~

Unfortunately, for the grandson, there wasn't anything that I could do. The young man is married

214

and owns property. Although the property is held jointly with his spouse, the IRS can still levy against his portion, and if he and his wife should file jointly, which they should as they have one child, then the IRS can grab any refund, unless the wife files an 'injured spouse form' to obtain her share of the refund.

The two of them felt that was too much trouble, so they agreed to pay the IRS the sum of $16,000 and change, on a monthly payment plan. The last payment was made in 2005.

~*~

One concern was the stock ownership of the corporation that owned the farm. Let's call it US-1. The corporation also would have a goodly amount of income, as the family had held a large quota.

It was decided that the stock for US-1 should be owned by a trust. That trust would be located in Belize. (You might guess that I had read David's book)

~*~

Belize, you may remember, is a small, underdeveloped country located in the Caribbean. Beautiful Caribbean country with a few most interesting laws.

Formerly known as British Honduras, the country has become a tax haven for many citizens from countries around the world. The laws of Belize are relatively lax, requiring only that the laws of Belize be

215

obeyed and that no individual engage in money laundering.

~*~

To establish an International Business Company or a Foreign Trust in Belize doesn't require personal appearances. Everything could be handled online, should one choose. In this case, I felt that it was incumbent on me to travel to Belize to choose the representative that I wanted to work with. His name was Eddie.

Eddie is a permanent resident of Belize, a repatriate originally from Texas. He had trouble with one branch of the U.S. government regarding selling securities, and decided that he would be better off outside the country. He had formed an association with attorneys in Belize and specialized in establishing International Business Companies (IBC's) and Foreign Trusts. Part of the requirement for having a Belize IBC or Foreign Trust was that a representative of the IBC or Trust must reside in Belize. Eddie filled that requirement.

With his assistance, I formed a trust to own the stock of US-1. Then I formed a second trust to be the beneficiary and the trustee of the first trust. After that, I formed an IBC to be the beneficiary of the second trust as well as the trustee of the second trust. Then, I formed an additional three IBC's.

One final act was to lease a small track of land (50 acres) at the cost of $1,000 per year. The purpose of the land was to have a foreign-based operation in the name of US-1.

The additional three IBC's would invoice US-1 for various amounts of monies for work done on the leased land in Belize. US-1 would pay those invoices by sending money to a bank account in a foreign bank that was jointly owned by the three IBC's. Because the IBC's were based in Belize, and the income was from invoices that covered 'work' performed on land in Belize, there was no income earned in the United States, so the IBC's didn't have to file a U.S. tax return. From this bank account, the monies would be transferred to a bank account owned by trust two.

Corporation US-1 would reduce its income by the amount of the invoices. This was permissible because U.S.-1 had joint operations in Belize and the United States. With the judicious uses of invoices the income of US-1 could be reduced to a point that only minimum corporate taxes ($450-$800) would have to be paid on a gross income near one million dollars.

Trust two would open a bank account in a foreign bank either based in the Bahamas, Belize or Panama. The trust would lend money to US-1 as needed, said loans not being income.

In order to obtain cash, debit cards were issued to Charles, David and Daddy.

Oh, by the way. During this entire operation, not one single law was broken in the United States. Nor were any of the Belizean laws were broken, either.

~*~

The leased land in Belize served another purpose, one that was completely legitimate. Charles had grown tired of the quotas that the United States Department of Agriculture had placed on tobacco growers. This was, of course, before the big buyout. Charles was certain that there must be somewhere in

217

the world where he could grow tobacco and import it into the United States without regards to a quota.

We decided, Charles and I, that we would approach the Belize government with the idea of growing tobacco in Belize. We would be able to rent as much land as we would need. There had been tobacco grown in Belize in years past, by a firm from South Africa. The firm had switched to growing oranges after their general manager and the tobacco expert had retired.

Charles had been using H-2A workers for a long time. H2-A workers are primarily Mexicans who come into the U.S. on a short-term visa to work in agriculture. One of the workers had been with Charles and his family for more than twenty years, returning to Mexico after the tobacco season and coming to the U.S. in the spring for planting. The Mexican agreed to oversee any tobacco operation in Belize.

Full of enthusiasm, I contacted a purchasing agent that was working for RJR, the tobacco giant. I informed him of our intent, and that we would be growing some fifty thousand pounds of tobacco. I felt that was a good round number. To my dismay, he laughed. Actually laughed at me.

Turns out that Reynolds would only be interested if I were talking about one million pounds.

Duh.

~*~

Okay! If plan A doesn't work, then it's on to plan B.

As I have said, Belize is an underdeveloped country of some 270,000 residents in a land area about the size of Rhode Island. There is no major crop other than sugar cane. With the world's use of sugar in the decline, land would be easily available.

Exports were virtually unknown. Papaya and bananas along with a few oranges were the exceptions. But with Eddie's help, we developed an alternative plan.

Habanera peppers grow extremely well in Belize. In fact, the soil in Belize, so rich from the burning of the cane stalks after harvest, is ideal for growing Habanera peppers and yields some hottest peppers in the world. Demand for the peppers to make hot sauce and for cosmetics keep the market price high. The focus thus changed from tobacco to hot peppers, watermelons, winter squash and other winter vegetables.

~*~

Charles's foreman, Miguel owned property in Mexico. He suggested that if we were going to consider growing vegetables, we should also consider Mexico. He stated that he had contacts there, many from his own family and the village where they lived, who would be willing to work with us and grow vegetables for us, if we would just provide the seeds and the materials. And of course, he would oversee the operation. For a small fee, that is.

Sounded reasonable to me.

~*~

While the farming operations were going on in Mexico and Belize, the tax program was also growing. Kyle's daughter-in-law was in charge of the Winston-Salem office, or so I thought. She had brought her brother to work in that office and it was her brother that did most of the managing. Unfortunately, the daughter-in law had found a new paramour.

William P. had resurfaced. Not wanting him to be too close to my office, I helped him locate office space in Mount Airy, North Carolina, where he would prepare income tax returns and send them by email to the Winston Salem office. There, all of the returns would be packaged and forwarded to my office and instantly forwarded to the software provider for filing with the IRS and the RAL bank.

It was my hope to limit the filing of any false income tax returns. I had already had a taste of the hospitality of the IRS and the Bureau of Prisons (BOP) and, frankly, I didn't want a repeat of the experience. Additionally, I didn't have too much faith in Kyle's daughter-in-law's brother, or in the daughter-in-law herself. She had performed well in the prior year, but now that she had left her husband and had moved in with William P., I was fearful that she might have changed. The fact that she became pregnant and would be delivering a child about the same time period that the tax-filing season would be in full swing, gave me additional concerns.

I reasoned that having the tax returns transmitted from my computer would provide additional security, whether I was in Mexico or Belize, or whether I was in my office. The refund checks were printed in my office and distributed to the other offices that had been designated by the tax-filer. That may well have been the worst decision of my life.

220

~*~

While this is not intended to be a recitation of the merits of growing and importing winter crops, I did promise to disclose everything.

With the help of a lawyer from Costa Rica, my son and I created a Limited Partnership, based in that country. The Limited Partnership owned Mexican companies that were involved in farming in Mexico and IBC's that were involved in farming in Belize.

Renting land and working with farmers in Mexico, we were successful in growing crops of cucumbers and watermelons for sale in the United States during the winter months of November, January, February and March.

We entered into contracts with several U.S. companies that wanted to purchase our fruit and vegetables. There was an agent in Mexico that worked with all of the companies, and we agreed to funnel everything through that agent.

The production of vegetables was very successful, as we shipped more than one million pounds of cucumbers and watermelons into Arizona and Texas. Receiving payment for the fruit and vegetables was a different matter.

We learned the lesson that many Mexican farmers had already learned. Having learned that lesson, the average Mexican farmer shuns any efforts of exportation and will sell much cheaper to local markets. We, or rather, I was unaware of the duplicity of mankind.

Wouldn't you think that being over sixty years old, and having had the experiences that I had to date, I would have learned something?

221

Duh.

Evidently, I hadn't.

When we would pack the fruit and vegetables into boxes and load them into trucks, the trucks would haul the produce to the border between the U.S. and Mexico. At that point, the produce would be loaded onto a truck or trailer from the United States and carried to a distribution point somewhere in the United States.

The agent would arrange for us to receive a 'pick and pack' payment. We would receive approximately $2.00 for a box of cucumbers weighing approximately 55 pounds.

At the time, cucumbers were selling for an average per box of $25.00. We would be paid $2.00 per box. The cost of the box was $1.00 per box. The cost of the freight was $1.75 per box. The miscellaneous costs of crossing the border, custom fees, etc would amount to $0.75 cents per box. Total cost that was to be deducted by the agent was $5.50 plus a ten percent sales commission. At the median price of $25.00 per box (some sold much higher and some slightly lower, depending on grade), the commission would be $2.50, making the total due the agent $8.00 per box. The remaining $17.00 should have been paid to my company and we were to be paid 90 days after shipping.

Sounds quite profitable, doesn't it?

Not!

Only after the produce had been packaged, shipped and sold, did the agent make any comments about some of the produce may have been sold at less than the market price. Without our permission, that action was completely illegal. At least, it was in the United States.

It was also illegal for the agent, who was a broker, to sell any produce to another broker. Seems like some people just want to break the rules.

The end result was that the broker defaulted on payments to our operation that could have amounted to as much as $600,000.00. The exact final figures are blurred because of events that were taking place in the United States and Belize.

~*~

During the past fifty years, the hurricanes that have crossed the Gulf of Mexico and the Caribbean Sea to hit Central America have not been all that numerous.

Not so while we were planting peppers. Three different times, the habanera pepper crops in Belize were destroyed by hurricanes that dumped copious amounts of water on the country.

Being a sub-tropic country, Belize receives a large amount of rain each year, but that is generally during the rainy season of August, September and early October. It is considered safe to plant in late October or November, with little chance of losing the crop to rain.

Hah.

Three consecutive years. Hurricanes. And rain. Floods, even.

Guess what?

That meant that the income from the income tax operation took on even more importance.

Still, the IRS dragon was about to roar one more time. And this time with a vengeance.

223

~*~

Kyle was proud of himself. He had lined up several clients who were operating legitimate businesses with substantial income. Some of those clients were used car dealers. Others were body shops, repair garages and junkyards.

Checking over one income-tax return with Kyle, I noted that the individual had claimed to have a repair shop that he operated from his home. That wasn't too unusual, as 'shade-tree' mechanics are plentiful in our area. One item came to my attention. A frame-bender.

Now, I don't really know what a frame bender is. I suppose that it is a machine that will straighten the frame on an automobile that has been involved in an accident. The thing that surprised me was how expensive one of those things was.

Kyle assured me that everything that he was doing was legitimate and correct, and that if one of his tax-filing clients claimed to have a repair-shop at home, the tax-filer did indeed have such an operation.

Kyle would go to the tax-filer's residence and pick up the papers and receipts necessary to prepare income tax returns. Once, as a lark – or possibly because I was a little skeptic – I rode with Kyle to one of his clients.

Sure enough, the client did have a repair shop at his home. (As an aside, when I had a 'fender bender' with my automobile, the man, Tracy, repaired my car, doing an excellent job). And there, in the shop, was a frame bender.

That didn't really calm my concerns regarding the income tax returns that Kyle was preparing, but he assured me repeatedly that he was following the straight and narrow, and that I shouldn't worry.

Easy for him to say, but much harder for me to do.

William P. had been joined by Kyle's now ex-daughter-in-law, Mary, at the tax office in Mt. Airy. I noticed the fees that William P. was putting on the tax return seemed to be quite large. When I asked the reason, William P. told me that the tax-filers that were paying the bigger fees were book-keeping clients of his and that the tax-filers had agreed for William P. to deduct the unpaid bookkeeping fees from the refund check.

I was aware that William P. was indeed the bookkeeper for a large number of small businesses, but I still wasn't reassured. Nonetheless, William P. was 55 miles from me, and I was certain that nothing that he was doing would rub off on me.

I insisted that William P. prepare receipts specifying the reason and the amount of each fee, feeling that those receipts would give me a security blanket.

Boy, was I wrong.

Big, big mistake. I would soon learn differently.

~*~

I was back in my comfort zone, forming International Business Companies and Foreign Trusts for a series of people. I was also forming domestic corporations for individuals who owned small businesses and who also wanted the asset protection of a corporation.

My son was also working with me as we set up a marketing company that would offer customer

225

incentive packages to businesses that were seeking additional clients.

Things were tight, as a result of the fiasco in Mexico, however, we were certain that we would eventually be able to collect at least the lion's share of the monies due us. Under the Texas Law, if a retail store purchased our cucumbers from a broker and we were not paid, the retail store could be held liable. Kyle had filed liens against all of the retail stores that we could document as having received our produce. We had not yet followed up on those liens, as the attorney in Texas wanted a fee of twenty-five thousand dollars in advance. And that was just the retainer. If I had been in possession of $25,000.00, I would have gladly put up the sum, despite having learned that it could take as much as five to seven years for the case to be resolved.

In the meanwhile, we needed more money than the tax preparation operation would yield, and I wasn't really needed as a tax preparer.

I developed a program for my son and I. We were marketing customer incentive bonus certificates to businesses that wanted to increase the number of their clients. The program was beginning to take off, as we had customers ranging from Connecticut to Georgia.

And right around the corner, a giant hammer was about to fall.

~*~

February 4, 2005.

I was in my office, working on projections for planting and farming in Mexico for the season that would begin in October 2005. It appeared that we would be successful in generating sufficient income that would enable us to plant several hundred acres, but not on the large scale that we had tried to before.

I had obtained an import-export license, made contacts with retail purchasers and was going to bypass the brokers. In this manner, I was certain that I would receive payment, both promptly and in full.

Kyle was in his office, three doors from mine. He was working on tax information for one of his business clients.

The telephone rang. Kyle answered and I could hear him tell the caller there was no Mr. Davis with our firm. Several minutes later, the front door opened and the SWAT team from the U.S. Marshall's office dashed inside. Swat teams with guns and bulletproof vests and leg irons. Leg irons and shackles that they were going to use on Kyle and me.

Can't you just imagine a couple of senior citizens (Kyle was 69 and I was 67) in handcuffs and shackles and leg irons? Made one hell of an impression on our neighbors.

One of the federal officers was a woman named Cathy. She had been the investigator on my earlier case, the one that I had infuriated. Even so, on the earlier occasion, she had just telephoned me and told me to report to the U.S. Marshall's office, an order that I obeyed.

I asked Cathy why the SWAT team on this occasion, and she told me that she wasn't in charge. I believe that she was embarrassed for the other federal officers. That is, if it's possible that a federal agent to be embarrassed.

Still, we were handcuffed, manacled, shackled, loaded into a federal automobile along with two guards each—we were dangerous people—and hauled away to the local pokey to be fingerprinted, mugged, and then released on our on recognizance.

227

~*~

I had been aware that I was the target of an investigation by the IRS for a couple of years. The investigators had been Cathy and her partner, Ted. Ted had refused to issue a warrant for me because he felt there was not sufficient evidence. Unfortunately for me, Ted retired and a new man was brought in. He wanted to clean up any old, incomplete investigations.

I wasn't worried in the slightest, as any returns that I had personally prepared should pass any audit. There had only been perhaps a half-dozen. There was absolutely zero fudging. I also presumed that I was remote enough from both Kyle and William P. that whatever they may have been doing would not reflect badly against me.

Another huge mistake. I had forgotten the lesson of my childhood companions blabbing to the sheriff.

Hey, look! It's not as if I had never encouraged my clients to lie, at worst, or at best, looked the other way when a client was lying. Those days were long gone. I had outgrown the need to build the business larger. And I didn't want a client repeating the action that old "Gone With The Wind" had executed. So, with a very few, well-trusted exceptions, my skirts were clean. And those few exceptions were well covered.

~*~

228

The charges against me personally were miniscule, even laughable.

I was accused of selling tax shelters, a bogus charge that was quickly dropped.

I was accused of filing a false income tax return for a female client from Rocky Mount, North Carolina. I did indeed pick up the papers and the receipts from the client and deliver them to the tax office in Winston Salem. After the tax return had been prepared, I did deliver the tax return back to the client in Rocky Mount for her signature and for her to mail. On the return, a mistake had been made. She had been listed as "Head of Household." She should have been listed as "Qualifying Widow", as a child must live in the house in order to qualify as "Head of Household." She had a child, but the child was married and living elsewhere. The net result of the mistake was that there was zero benefit to the tax-filer, and when there is no monetary loss under the Internal Revenue Code there is no crime.

I was accused of filing a false tax return for a man who lived in King, North Carolina. It is very likely that I did at least help prepare that tax return. We had opened an office in King, sharing space with a business owner, and the business owner wanted to learn to prepare taxes using one of our computers and our software. I agreed to teach him, and worked with three or four tax-filers, showing the businessman, Dave, how to complete a tax return. I really don't remember if it were Dave or I who prepared the tax return, but on the return, the tax-filer was inadvertently listed as "Head of Household" instead of the proper filing status of "Single." The monetary difference, the tax-filer received an extra $24.00. Twenty-four dollars. I'm firmly convinced that regardless of whether Dave or I

229

prepared the return, no one would cheat on a tax return for the sum of $24.00.

Duh!

But, the IRS wasn't about to let me get away free.

The final charge was Conspiracy to Defraud the United States Government.

~*~

Told you that conspiracy was a real mother.

Conspiracy along with Kyle and William P. to defraud the U.S. Government.

My self-imposed security distancing didn't seem to be too effective.

Of course, I immediately yelled for a lawyer.

~*~

While the charges against me may have been miniscule, the charges against Kyle and William P. were much more severe. Kyle was faced with fifteen charges and William P. was slapped with nine.

Certain facts began to surface. Among the nine tax returns that William P. was charged with falsifying, one was for his cousin. This cousin, according to the income tax return that William P. had prepared, was the owner of a beauty salon. Losses had occurred in the business, again according to the tax return, and the losses had enabled the cousin to claim a fairly substantial tax refund, including the maximum amount of Earned Income Tax Credit.

William P. had charged her $750.00 for preparing and filing the tax return. He assured me that the fee was because he was the beauty salon's bookkeeper. The cousin objected to the fee, but William P. told her that she had gotten back extra money and that she had actually received five hundred dollars extra because of his efforts. He refused to give her additional money. She was still angry, and notified the IRS that something was not quite right.

The cousin and eight other clients for whom William P. had prepared returns were prepared to testify that William P. had falsified their returns and had collected large, unearned fees.

The U.S. Prosecuting Attorney hinted there were even many more of William P.'s clients who had been so victimized.

Things looked dark for William P.

~*~

If things looked dark for William P., the situation for Kyle was as black as ink. While he had been charged with preparing fifteen false income tax returns, the U.S. Prosecuting Attorney stated that there were at least fifty-four tax-filers who would testify that Kyle had personally prepared their tax returns and that he had falsified the information on the return. (Without their knowledge or help, of course).

Another charge against Kyle was that he had delivered false documents to the IRS auditor. Receipts that Kyle had presented on behalf of a client who was being audited were found to be completely false, fabricated by an individual or individuals unknown. Turned out that particular client was a cousin of Kyle's wife. And, of course, the client told the IRS

231

investigators that the client had no knowledge of Kyle's activities on their behalf and they had not provided the receipts for business expenses. In fact, the client told the IRS that the client had no business venture at all, and that Kyle must have fabricated any and all information relating to business and deductions on the tax return.

Without their knowledge or participation, of course. Right!

Yet, they were pleased to cash the sizable tax refund check.

No knowledge? No participation?

Duh.

~*~

Let me set the scene so that it is a little more understandable. Here we were: one person—Kyle— almost seventy years old. Remember his age, because it becomes important later. More than fifty-five of his clients were willing to testify in court that Kyle had fabricated false information on their tax returns; information which they didn't furnish and didn't comprehend why it was listed in the first place. Seems like all of those clients had been audited and were required to make reimbursements of the excess refunds to the IRS. Facing fifty-five hostile witnesses, Kyle could easily have been charged with fifty-five false returns, rather than the fifteen with which he was charged. That would mean a long time in prison, as the severity of the sentence imposed by the Judge is partly based upon the monetary loss created by the false returns.

At Kyle's age, that would be the same as a life sentence.

232

And then there was William P. William P. was a sixty-year old man with a new live-in playmate and a recently born child. In addition to the nine charges he was facing, there were roughly twenty others who had also agreed to testify. To add to William P's difficulties, he had a lengthy record, having been in prison on more than one occasion. He had also been convicted many times for Driving While Under the Influence of Drugs or Alcohol, and another factor in considering how long to sentence anyone to prison is their prior record. William P's prior record was a lulu.

Can you believe that he might have gotten a rather lengthy prison sentence?

My situation was that two minor mistakes had been made; if not by me, then by someone I supervised. The total potential loss would have been $24.00. There was no one to testify that I had prepared any tax return at all, much less one that contained false information.

Looked like I was sitting pretty, didn't it?

Guess again.

~*~

Remember that conspiracy thing?

Although court appointed attorneys had been assigned to represent Kyle and myself, I was certain that there was an attorney that would be able to defeat the IRS more easily than the one appointed by the court. That may or may not have been true, but it was my justification in hiring the legal expert who is considered the top-rated local attorney that practiced in the federal courts.

233

My attorney hired a retired executive of the IRS as an expert witness-the one that I mentioned earlier. The expert, who had been the head of the North Carolina division of the IRS, listened to the story about the clients being ignorant about entries made by Kyle and William P. on their tax returns with bemusement. His comment was included earlier in this recital. He stated that in some 20,000 cases handled while he was the head IRS officer in the State, the tax-filer never, repeat never, was aware that there was any incorrect information on the tax return.

He stated that the two charges against me should never had been filed and both he and my attorney were one-hundred percent certain that I would not be found guilty of any wrong-doing, if we should go to trial.

Be reminded that this attorney was retained to represent me and only me. Another was retained to represent Kyle and William P. had an attorney representing him.

A conference between my attorney and the U.S. Prosecuting Attorney revealed that the U.S. attorney was absolutely certain that I was the ringleader, the mastermind of IRS fraud in Winston-Salem and High Point. Perhaps, even in the entire state of North Carolina. He wasn't about to dismiss the charges against me, despite the lack of evidence. He further stated that he intended to go after Kyle and William P. for the projected loss of two million dollars or more, as the Judge would allow him to estimate how many tax returns had been prepared by the two of them, and under the conspiracy, it was possible that I might be convicted, as well.

Still, I was determined to fight. I was certain that there were no false or intentionally dishonest income tax returns prepared by me. And, if Kyle and

William P. had filed false returns, it wasn't because of my actions.

Sounds good doesn't it? It sounded good to me at the time. Didn't work out quite that way.

Damn.

~*~

My attorney and his partners asked for a conference with the tax expert witness and me. The door was closed and we were completely open and honest with one another. It was agreed by everyone that I could easily beat the charges that had been logged against me, except for the possibility of one. That one was the conspiracy.

In the law's eyes, conspiracy is not necessarily the act of assisting in preparing false returns, but if one knows – OR SHOULD HAVE KNOWN –that false returns were being prepared, even if they were never filed, then that person may well be convicted under the conspiracy law.

My attorney reminded me that because I owned all of the leases on the different tax offices, all of the furniture and the computers, all of the software, and that I insisted on handling all of the money, I was open to a jury determining that, at least, I should have known.

One of the partner attorneys asked me how much faith I had in Kyle and William P. I had to be frank. I trusted Kyle much more than William P. but was certain that each would watch out for his own self.

The attorney asked if I thought they would do what was in their own best interest, and again I had to admit that they would, especially William P.

The attorney then asked me to think just a moment. Would Kyle, at 70 years of age, testify that I didn't know what he was doing and accept a lengthy prison sentence, possibly as much as seven years or longer, or would he perhaps cut a deal with the Prosecuting Attorney to testify that I knew all about his misdeeds in return for a reduced sentence of only one year or less?

Another partner asked me almost the exact same question about William P. Would he testify that I was remote and unknowledgeable about his operation, or would he testify that I was indeed aware of the techniques he was using to generate the large fees he was receiving? If he testified that I did not know, he was subject to a prison sentence of eight years to fifteen years. Would he lie to get a shorter sentence, possibly only three years?

Duh!

Added to the consideration that I had to make was the provable fact that I received all of the tax returns the two men had prepared and had transmitted them to the Internal Revenue Service. Although I would not have been able to review them or change the returns in any way, nevertheless, I was the transmitting agent.

What would a jury believe?

Would the jury believe me, saying I didn't do it, with my record of already having pled guilty once before? Or, would the jury believe that I had transmitted the returns knowing they contained false information? And what would the jury think about the fact that I owned everything and controlled all of the money and wrote all of the checks? Could the jury believe that I was actually innocent?

And then, consider the fact it was likely that Kyle didn't want to go to prison for five to seven years at his age. He had a bad heart, diabetes, and other illnesses that required him to take twenty-six pills every day. Being in prison that long could have fatal results. How would he testify?

And William P. Facing eight to fifteen years in prison and being away from his new lover. How would he testify?

The protective shield that I believed that I had intentionally built around me was becoming less secure.

What would you have done?

~*~

No one has ever accused me of being a rocket scientist, or Einstein. But, on the other hand, I have never been accused of being Mortimer Snerd. (For you younger people, that was the name of one of Edgar Bergen's dummies. You know, Edgar Bergen, the ventriloquist. Oh, well, it's an old folks joke.)

Yes, I could see the handwriting on the wall. And, yes, I was certain that either one or the other of the two would be willing to include me in order to receive a much lighter sentence.

My attorney informed me that if one or the other of them, and likely both, testified that I was in a position to have known about any false information, I would be convicted, and that the U.S. Prosecuting Attorney was trying to have me sentenced to a minimum of 120 months (ten years).

Ouch!

Damn.

~*~

Time to get my head out of the clouds. There was no way that I would walk away clean, so I had to look at other options. Although I had prided myself of being a member of MENSA, there were many, many times when I did indeed feel exactly like Mortimer Snerd. For a supposedly intelligent man, I was certainly stupid. This was one of those times.

Of course, it wasn't possible to be in my position and not suspect that both Kyle and William P. were doing things to enhance the returns that they were preparing on behalf of their clients. Truthfully, they were too eager to please their clients, or too greedy in their deductions. While not knowing the details of exactly what they were doing, I felt sure they were manipulating numbers, but I though I had shielded myself against any possible exposure. It was time to get real.

~*~

Looking for the best situation, it was proposed that, if I would plead guilty to conspiracy and advise Kyle and William P to plead guilty to the same charge, that William P would receive a sentence of 42 months, which could be reduced to as little as 24 months by undergoing drug rehabilitation while in prison. Kyle would be sentenced to 13 months, and would spend 11 months in prison and two months at home.

The best I could hope for was a sentence of fifteen months, and I would have to spend twelve months in prison. That tasted bitter, but the alternative, should we fight in court and lose, my sentence may well be ten years. Not too smart, but not especially dumb either.

238

Guess which I chose?
You got that one right again.
I chose the easy route.

~*~

Frankly, it was so easy to persuade Kyle and William P to agree, that I am certain one or both of them had already spoken with the prosecuting attorney about testifying against me.

~*~

That's the way it came down. As I walked from the courtroom, preparing to report to the Federal Bureau of Prisons System, I could hear the U.S. Prosecuting Attorney berating the Judge, insisting that I was the mastermind and, as such, deserved to spend at least ten years in prison and I was walking away with just a year.

Boy, I'm glad that lawyer wasn't the Judge.

(By the way, Beckley, West Virginia is no better than Butner, North Carolina, and the Corrections Officers (guards) are even weirder)

Tricks of an IRS Cheat and other Scandals../Connor

240

Can't Sweat The Small Stuff

Before ending, a few items for you to reflect
on:

- Among the many superlatives
associated with Hurricane Katrina can now be
added this one: it produced one of the most
extraordinary displays of scams, schemes and
stupefying bureaucratic bungles in modern
history, costing taxpayers up to $2 billion.
- A hotel owner in Sugar Land,
Tex., has been charged with submitting
$232,000.00 in bills for phantom victims. And
roughly 1,100 prison inmates across the Gulf
Coast have apparently collected more than $10
million in rental and disaster-relief assistance.
- There are bureaucrats who
ordered nearly a half a billion dollars worth of
mobile homes that are still empty, and
renovations for a shelter at a former Alabama
Army base that cost about $416,000 per
evacuee.
- And there is the Illinois woman
who tried to collect federal benefits by claiming
she watched her two daughters drown in the
rising New Orleans waters. In fact, prosecutors
say, the children did not exist.

The estimate of up to $2 billion in fraud
and waste represents nearly 11 percent of the
$19 billion spent by FEMA on Hurricanes
Katrina and Rita as of mid-June,, or about 6

percent of the total money that has been obligated.

~New York Times 06-27-2006~

Twelve different government agencies enforce thirty-five different food-safety laws and the GAO says that the responsibilities are so fragmented that tax payers are being fleeced - even hurt. Every year up to eighty cases of illnesses come from bad food at a cost of up to $37 billion. No big surprise there. For many years our government has enjoyed it's free spending habits without the same restraints that we, the taxpayers, and the ones they GET the money from, do not, nor will we ever, have. The GAO's high-risk list seems to be agencies that seem unwilling or unable to change or solve the problems. The number of problem agencies on the GAO's list has nearly doubled since it's inception in 1990. In 1990, there were a total of fourteen agencies on the GAO's list to twenty-six in 1999. Over that time period, eighteen programs were added, but only six were removed. Ten of these problem agencies have been on the list since it began over a decade ago. So where are we being fleeced? Let's take a look.

Management at the DOE (Department of Energy)

is so disjointed that radioactive tritium has leaked into ground water and that clean up of radioactive waste at the site where the leakage is occurring is twenty six months behind schedule and $200 million over budget!

Transportation Department

The GAO estimates that the FAA has wasted $1 1/2 million in its seventeen-year effort to modernize the air traffic control.

Department of Housing & Urban Development

Management waste in disposing of HUD single family housing inventory is costing taxpayers over $1 million every day! The GAO has listed the entire agency on it's high risk list.

Department of Health and Human Services

Medicare - the Inspector General at the Department of Health and Human Services found over $20 billion in improper payments in Medicare's Fee-For-Service Program. That represents 11% of the entire Fee-For-Service Program!

Food Stamps

Almost $1 billion a year is lost because of improper food stamp payments. The average American would be outraged to know that his or her tax dollars are paying for food stamps for prisoners, fugitive felons and people who are dead, not to mention the enormous amounts of illegal immigrants who flood the gates on a daily basis.

The IRS

The largest seedbed for fraud found in the IRS is the various tax credit programs. The largest by far is the Earned Income Tax Credit Program. In 1995, the EIC program alone sustained $4.4 billion in over claims! This figure represents over 25% of the total claims of this program, that's right 25%!

The Social Security Administration Supplemental Security Income (SSI)

This program is supposed to provide cash benefits to the blind and the disabled children & adults. This program suffers from long-standing abuse, mismanagement, & increasing overpayments to those who don't deserve them - $1 billion for fiscal year 1998 and about $3.3 billion cumulatively. These overpayments are going to convicted felons, prisoners, people who are in this country illegally but the most disturbing part of the SSI's overpayments are to individuals who make claim to the program that they caused themselves such as alcoholics and drug abuses. These people choose the road their lives were going to take, why should the taxpayers pay for the drunken man down the street to sit at home and drink more? Why should the taxpayers pay for the drug user to get high everyday? A disgusting misuse of our funds.

Enough!
Please!

~Finale~

Before you begin feeling pity for me, know that I have done enough that the punishments that I have received may well be less than I deserve. But, be that as it may .

You know how 'they' are always asking, "Do you have any final comments?"

Well, yeah, I suppose that I do.

At a weak moment, I voluntarily reached an agreement with the Internal Revenue Service whereby I would not personally prepare any income tax returns in the future. Nor would I personally be transmitting any tax returns. That agreement was made on behalf Bill Jackson.

But, study carefully the information about corporations, IBC's and offshore trusts and how they conceal ownership.

Duh!

Can you say, "Consultant?"

My final comment? "Psst. Hey, buddy! Can you spare a tax break?"

~Addendum~

Just When You Thought the IRS Couldn't Be Humorous
(A collection of quotes, misquotes and sayings)

For your fun and amusement, don't take it too seriously.
A word of warning; some of these may sting. (P.S. Some of these have already been used before, but we like them. Hope you do.)

~*~

Dear Sirs:

I am responding to your letter denying the deduction for two of the three dependents I claimed on my 1994 Federal Tax return. Thank you. I have questioned whether these are my children for years. They are evil and expensive. It's only fair that since they are minors and not my responsibility that the government (who evidently is taxing me more to care for these waifs) knows something about them and what to expect over the next year. You may apply next year to reassign them to me and reinstate the deduction. This year, they are yours!

The oldest, Kristen, is now 17. She is brilliant. Ask her. I suggest you put her to work in your office where she can answer people's questions about their returns. While she has no formal training, it has not seemed to hamper her knowledge of any other subject you can name. Taxes should be a breeze. Next year she is going to college. I think it's wonderful that you will now be responsible for that little expense. While you mull that over, keep in mind she has a truck. It doesn't run at the moment, so you have the immediate decision of appropriating some Department of Defense funds to fix the vehicle or getting up early to drive her to school. Kristen also has a boyfriend. Oh, joy. While she possesses all the wisdom of the universe, her alleged mother and I have felt it best to occasionally remind her of the virtues of abstinence, and in the face of overwhelming passion, safe sex. This is always uncomfortable and I am quite relieved you will be handling this in the future. May I suggest that you reinstate Jocelyn Elders who had a rather good handle on the problem?

Patrick is 14. I've had my suspicions about this one. His eyes are a little close together for normal people. He may be a tax examiner himself one day, if you do not incarcerate him first. In February, I was awakened at three in the morning by a police officer that was bringing Pat home. He and his friends were TP'ing houses. In the future would you like him delivered to the local IRS office or to Ogden, UT? Kids at 14 will do almost anything on a dare. His hair is purple. Permanent dye, temporary dye, what's the big deal? Learn to deal with it. You'll have plenty of time as he is sitting out a few days of school after instigating a food fight. I'll take care of filing your phone number with the vice principal. Oh yes, he and his friends have raging hormones. This is a house of testosterone and it will be much more peaceful when he lives in your home. **Do not** leave any of them unsupervised with girls, explosives, inflammables, inflatables, vehicles or

251

telephones. (I'm sure that you will find telephones a source of unimaginable amusement, and be sure to lock out the 900 and 976 numbers!)

Heather is an alien. She slid through a time warp and appeared quite by magic one year. I'm sure this one is yours. She is 10 going on 21. She came from a bad trip in the sixties. She wears tie-dyed clothes, beads, sandals, and hair that looks like Tiny Tim's. Fortunately you will be raising my taxes to help offset the pinch of her remedial reading courses. Hooked On Phonics is expensive so the schools dropped it. Good news! You can buy it yourself for half the amount of the deduction that you are denying! It's quite obvious that we were terrible parents (ask the other two) so they have helped raise this one to a new level of terror. She cannot speak English. Most people under twenty understand the curious patois she fashioned out of valley girls/boys in the hood/reggae/yuppie/ political doublespeak. I don't. The school sends her to a speech pathologist that has her roll her R's. It added a refreshing Mexican/Irish touch to her voice. She wears hats backwards, pants baggy and wants one of her ears pierced four more times. There is a fascination with tattoos that worries me but I am sure that you can handle it. Bring a truck when you come to get her, she sort of "nests" in her room and I think that it would be easier to move the entire thing than find out what it is really made of.

You denied two of the three exemptions so it is only fair you get to pick which two you will take. I prefer that you take the youngest. I'll still go bankrupt with Kristen's college but then I am free. If you take the two oldest, then I still have time for counseling before Heather becomes a teenager. If you take the two

252

girls then I won't feel so bad about putting Patrick in a military academy. Please let me know of your decision as soon as possible, as I have already increased the withholding on my W-4 to cover the $395 in additional tax and made a down payment on an airplane.

Yours Truly,

Bob

(**Note:** The taxpayer in question added this caveat at a later date. "Rats, they sent me the refund and allowed the deductions." Our response, "Gee, Bob, sometimes you just can't get a break.")

~*~

Interactive Tax Software

Hello! Welcome to Taxtime, your Interactive Tax Preparer Program. Do you feel like doing your taxes today?

I see. Well, don't you think you should do them anyway? After all, it is April 7th. You have less than 10 days to file. And who knows? Maybe you'll get a refund.

That's the spirit! Let's begin with your name, address, and marital status.

Sorry to hear about the divorce. But don't let it get you down ... That alimony deduction will come in mighty handy in these tough financial times!

Please don't cry. The economy's bound to bounce back. In the meantime, let's talk about dependents. Do you have any children?

Wow! I hope they're not all in college. Do you have any other dependents?

Sorry. You can't deduct your dog, even if she is your only friend.

I agree. The IRS is unreasonable. But let's move on to income. What were your wages last year?

You **are** having a bad go of it, aren't you? But at least you're getting the Unemployment Benefits max.

I'm afraid Unemployment Benefits **are** taxable. The government giveth and the government taketh away. **Hey**, don't blame me. I'm just the messenger.

Anyway, did you have any interest or dividend income or capital gains?

Your spouse got everything, huh? Well, look on the bright side. If you don't earn it, they can't make you pay taxes on it.

Please don't leave. It was just a joke. I don't suppose you were able to sock anything away into an IRA?

254

I didn't mean to insult you. I'm just doing my job. They make me ask about IRA's and Keogh Plans, too.

Okay, okay. I get the point. **You're broke.** So let's go over your deductions and see about getting you a healthy refund. And speaking about health, I need a complete list of your non- reimbursed medical expenses.

That's great -- a fractured sacroiliac. And your income was so low that most of it will be deductible! Let's move on to your state income taxes and real estate taxes.

Boy, those state taxes can really take a bite, eh? But that huge mortgage tax deduction should really increase your refund.

What? You had to sell the house to pay for the divorce? What a shame. But I thought you said you didn't have any capital gains.

You sold it at a loss? Really? So tell me ... Do you think housing is going to drop any further? One of my co-workers is looking to buy.

You're absolutely right. That was a selfish and thoughtless thing to say. I'm a new program, and I guess they haven't gotten all the bugs out.

Let's go back to your deductions. What did you pay in mortgage interest?

I'm afraid deducting credit card interest is a major no-no. But you may want to consider our Interactive Bankruptcy Software!

Hey, now. Don't get your nose out of joint. It was just a suggestion. Anyway, it's time to list your charitable contributions. I know you can't afford them, but list a couple hundred in cash anyway. Everybody does it, and it's impossible to check.

Good. Now I'm almost afraid to ask, but did you suffer any unreimbursed casualty or theft losses last year?

That's pretty much what I expected. Just give me the numbers and I'll take it from there.

Is there anything else you want to tell me?

I'm sorry; I don't really have time to listen about your divorce anymore. What I meant was, did you have any other income or expenses? Fine. Now why don't you rest for a second, so I can do some quick calculations?

I have good news. You're entitled to a $157 refund. Would you like to apply it to your tax for next year?

I beg your pardon. They don't pay me enough to listen to that kind of language.

~*~

Will Rogers

- After eating an entire bull, a mountain lion felt so good he started roaring. He kept it up until a hunter came along and shot him. **The moral:** When you're full of bull, keep your mouth shut.
- Always drink upstream from the herd.
- Don't squat with your spurs on.
- Good judgment comes from experience, and a lot of that comes from bad judgment.
- I don't make jokes. I just watch the government and report the facts.
- I don't want to complain but every time they build a tax structure, the first thing they nail is I!
- I love a dog. He does nothing for political reasons.
- If there are no dogs in Heaven, then when I die I want to go where they went.
- If you find yourself in a hole, the first thing to do is stop diggin'.
- If you get to thinkin' you're a person of some influence, try orderin' somebody else's dog around.
- If you're ridin' ahead of the herd, take a look back every now and then to make sure it's still there.
- Income tax has made more liars out of the American people than golf. (And, here's a story about Will Rogers and his income tax:

Will Rogers, having paid too much income tax one year, tried in vain to claim a rebate. His numerous letters and queries remained unanswered. Eventually

257

the form for the next year's return arrived. In the section marked **Deductions**, Rogers listed:

Bad debt, US Government -- $40,000

- It don't take a genius to spot a goat in a flock of sheep.
- Lettin' the cat outta the bag is a whole lot easier 'n puttin' it back in.
- Lord, the money we do spend on Government and it's not one bit better than the government we got for one-third the money twenty years ago.
- Never kick a cow chip on a hot day.
- Never miss a good chance to shut up.
- Never slap a man who's chewin' tobacco.
- On account of being a democracy and run by the people, we are the only nation in the world that has to keep a government four years, no matter what it does.
- The quickest way to double your money is to fold it over and put it back in your pocket.
- There are two theories to arguin' with a woman. Neither one works.
- When you give a lesson in meanness to a critter or a person, don't be surprised if they learn their lesson.
- When you're throwin' your weight around, be ready to have it thrown around by somebody else.

~*~

Scam Alert

Warning! Please Read Immediately This is Serious!

If you get an envelope from a company called the "Internal Revenue Service," **do not open it!** This group operates a scam around this time every year.

Their letter claims that you owe them money, which they will take and use to pay for the operation of essential functions of the United States government.

This is untrue! The money the IRS collects is used to fund various other corporations, which depend on subsidies to stay in business.

This organization has ties to another shady outfit called the Social Security Administration, who claim to take money from your regular paychecks and save it for your retirement. In truth, the SSA uses the money to pay for the same misguided corporate welfare the IRS helps mastermind.

These scam artists have bilked honest, hard working Americans out of billions of dollars. Don't be among them!

Forward this message to everyone you know!

259

~*~

The Wages of Sin

A man named Tony died, one day. When he stood before the throne to be judged, he was told that he had committed a sin and so he could not go to Heaven right away. His sin was cheating on his income taxes and the only way he could get into heaven was to sleep with an ugly woman for the next five years and enjoy it. Tony decided, this was a small price to pay for an eternity in Heaven. So, off he went with the ugly woman, pretending to be happy.

As he was walking along, he saw his friend Carlos up ahead. Carlos was with an even uglier woman than Tony. When he approached Carlos, he asked him what was going on. Carlos answered, "I cheated on my income taxes and scammed the government out of a lot of money ... even more then you did."

They both shook their heads in understanding and figured that as long as they had to be with these women, they might as well hang out together to help pass the time.

Now Tony, Carlos and their two beastly women were walking along, minding their own business, when Tony and Carlos could have sworn that they saw their friend Jon up ahead. Only this man was with an absolutely drop-dead gorgeous supermodel/centerfold. Stunned, Tony and Carlos approached the man and in fact it was their friend Jon. They asked him, why was he with this unbelievable

260

goddess, while they were stuck with these awful women.

Jon replied, "I have no idea, and I'm definitely not complaining. This has been absolutely the best time of my life. I am looking forward to five years of the best sex any man could hope for. There is only one thing that I can't seem to understand. After every time we have sex, she rolls over and murmurs to herself ..."

*(%$!:} income taxes!!!!!

~*~

A certain tax attorney took on a very complex case of tax evasion for a rather mysterious client. He devoted over a year to the case, familiarizing himself with every loophole and angle of current legislation, and made a brilliant argument before the court. His client was called out of town when the jury returned with its verdict, a sweeping victory for his client on every count. Flushed with victory, the lawyer exuberantly cabled his client, "Justice has triumphed!"

A realistic fellow, the client immediately wired back, "Appeal at once!"

~*~

The IRS Agent on Halloween
261

The door bell rings, and a man answers it.

Here stands this plain but well dressed kid, saying, "Trick or Treat!"

The man asks the kids what he is dressed up like for Halloween.

The kid replies, "I'm an IRS agent."

Then he takes 40 percent of the man's candy, leaves, and doesn't say thank you.

~*~

Q: How is golf like taxes?
A: Well, you drive hard to get to the green, and then you wind up in the hole.

~*~

Bartender & IRS Agent

The local bar was so sure that its bartender was the strongest man around that they offered a standing $1000 bet. The bartender would squeeze a lemon until all the juice ran into a glass, and hand the lemon to a patron. Anyone who could squeeze one more drop of juice out would win the money. Many people had tried over time (weight-lifters, longshoremen, etc.) but nobody could do it.

One day this scrawny little man came into the bar, wearing thick glasses and a polyester suit, and said in a tiny squeaky voice.

"I'd like to try the bet." After the laughter had died down, the bartender said OK, grabbed a lemon, and squeezed away. Then he handed the wrinkled remains of the rind to the little man.

But the crowd's laughter turned to total silence as the man clenched his fist around the lemon and six drops fell into the glass. As the crowd cheered, the bartender paid the $1000, and asked the little man.

"What do you do for a living? Are you a lumberjack, a weight-lifter, what?"

The man replied, "I work for the IRS."

~*~

"It's income tax time again, Americans: time to gather up those receipts, get out those tax forms, sharpen up that pencil, and stab yourself in the aorta."
-- D. Barry

263

~*~

A fool and his money are soon parted. It takes creative tax laws for the rest.
-- C Bob Thaves

~*~

The invention of the teenager was a mistake. Once you identify a period of life in which people get to stay out late but don't have to pay taxes naturally, no one wants to live any other way.
-- Judith Martin (writing as "Miss Manners")

~*~

I have always paid income tax. I object only when it reaches a stage when I am threatened with having nothing left for my old age - which is due to start next Tuesday or Wednesday.
-- Noel Coward

~*~

What's the difference between an optimist, a
pessimist, and an accountant?
To the optimist, the glass of water is half full.
To the pessimist, the glass of water is half empty.
To the accountant, the glass of water is twice as big as
it needs to be.

~*~

The Internal Revenue Code is about 10 times
the size of the Bible - and unlike the Bible, contains no
good news.
-- Don Rickles

~*~

We'll try to cooperate fully with the IRS,
because, as citizens, we feel a strong patriotic duty not
to go to jail.
-- Dave Barry

~*~

Avoid strong drink. It can cause you to shoot at
tax collectors...and miss!
-- Robert A. Heinlein

~*~

"What this country needs is a really good five-cent cigar."
-- Thomas Riley Marshall (VP of the USA 1913-1921)

"There are plenty of good five
cent cigars in this country. The problem
is they cost a quarter. What this country
needs is a good five cent nickel."
-- W.C. Fields response to above quote

~*~

When Congress talks of tax reform, grab your wallet and run for cover.
---Senator Steve Symms, Idaho

~*~

"In the last decade, taxes have been raised four times explicitly for deficit reduction. In the year following each hike, the deficit actually increased."
---Senator Dan Coats

266

~*~

"Politicians tax the middle class for the same reason that some people rob banks. That's where the money is."

---Forbes Magazine, May 11, 1992

~*~

"If our current tax structure were a TV show, it would either be 'Foul-ups, Bleeps and Blunders,' or 'Gimme a Break'. If it were a record album, it would be 'Gimme Shelter.'

If it were a movie, it would be 'Revenge of the Nerds' or maybe 'Take the Money and Run.' And if the IRS ever wants a theme song, maybe they'll get Sting to do 'Every breath you take, every move you make, I'll be watching you.'"

---President Ronald Regan, Northside High School, Atlanta, GA, June 6, 1985

~*~

"And to you taxpayers out there, let me say this: Make sure you file your tax return on time! And

remember that, even though income taxes can be a
'pain in the neck,' the folks at the IRS are regular
people just like you, except that they can destroy your
life.
-- Dave Barry

~*~

"Vice President Dick Cheney's getting a tax
refund of $1.9 million. How do you get a $1.9 million
refund when your salary is $205,000 a year? How does
that work?...Apparently, he's writing off the guns and
ammo as business expenses."....Jay Leno

~*~

A new arrival, about to enter hospital, saw two
white-coated doctors searching through the flowerbeds.

268

"Excuse me," he said. "Have you lost something?"

"No," replied one of the doctors. "We're doing a heart transplant for an income-tax auditor and want to find a suitable stone."

~*~

"65% of people say that cheating on your income tax is worse than cheating on your spouse. The other 35% were women."...Jay Leno

~*~

A couple of weeks after hearing a sermon on Psalms 51: 2-4 and Psalms 52: 3-4 (lies and deceit), a man wrote the following letter to the IRS:

"I have been unable to sleep, knowing that I cheated on my income tax. I understated my taxable income, and have enclosed a check for $250.00.

Sincerely, Taxpayer

P.S. If I still can't sleep, I'll send the rest.

269

~*~

Why does a slight tax increase cost you two hundred dollars and a substantial tax cut save you thirty cents?

~*~

Fight back! Fill out your tax forms with Roman numerals.

~*~

Did you ever notice? When you put the two words "the" and "IRS" together, it spells "theirs?"

~*~

A visitor from Holland was chatting with his American friend and was jokingly explaining about the red, white and blue in the Netherlands flag.

"Our flag symbolizes our taxes," he said. "We get red when we talk about them, white when we see our tax bill, and blue after we pay them."

"That's the same with us," the American said, "Only we see stars, too."

~*~

When you do a good deed, get a receipt...in case Heaven is like the IRS.

~*~

"I hate to be the one to remind you, but just pretty soon it is going to be April 15th, it is going to be tax time. You know what I am saying? Are you ready? Well, you know when something like this happens, New Yorkers always try to put the best face they can on a situation. For example, the hookers in Times Square, for an extra $50, they will handle your extension."   ......David Letterman

271

~*~

HOW TO ANNOY THE IRS (Without getting into trouble)

Well, it is tax time again, boys and girls. So cough it up if you haven't already! But, no one says you have to go gently into that dark night. Here are some hints on how to bug the IRS if you owe them money...

1. Always put staples in the right hand corner. Go ahead and put them down the whole right side. The extractors who remove the mail from the envelopes have to take out all of the staples on the right side.

2. Never arrange paperwork in the right order, or even facing the same way. Put a page or two upside down and backwards. That way they have to remove all of your staples, rearrange all of the paperwork and re-staple it (on the left side).

3. Line the bottom of your envelope with Elmer's glue and let it dry before you put in your forms, so that the automated opener doesn't open it and the extractor has to open it by hand.

4. If you're very unfortunate and have to pay taxes, use a two or three party check. On top of paying with a third party check, pay one of the dollars you owe in cash. When the extractor receives cash, no matter how small an amount, he or she has to take it to a special desk and fill out a few nasty forms.

272

5. Write a little letter of appreciation. Any letter received has to be read and stamped regardless of what it is or what it's on.

6. Write your setter on something misshapen and unconventional. Like on the back of a Kroger sack.

7. When you mail it, mail it in a big envelope (even if it is just a single EZ form). Large envelopes have to be torn and sorted differently than regular business size ones. An added bonus to the big envelope is that they take priority over other mail, so the IRS workers can hurry up and deal with your mess.

8. If you send two checks, they'll have to staple your unsightly envelope to your hand-destroyed form.

9. Always put extra paper clips on your forms. Any foreign fasteners or the like have to be removed and put away.

10. Sign your name in ink on every page. Any signature has to be verified and then date stamped.

These are just of the few of the fun and exciting things you can do with the IRS. These methods are **only** recommended if you owe money.

~*~

A man had fallen between the rails in a subway station. People were all crowding around trying to get him out before the train ran him over. They were all shouting, "Give me your hand!" But the man would not reach up.

Joe elbowed his way through the crowd and leaned over the man. "Friend," he asked, "What is your profession?"

"I am an income tax inspector," gasped the man.

"In that case," said Joe, "Take my hand!"

The man immediately grasped the Joe's hand and was hauled to safety. Joe turned to the amazed by-standers and declared, "Never ask a tax man to *give* you anything, you fools!"

~*~

TAXPAYER'S LAMENT

Tax his cow, Tax his goat;
Tax his pants, Tax his coat;
Tax his crop, Tax his work;
Tax his ties, Tax his shirt;

Tax his chew, Tax his smoke (now ain't that the truth);
Teach him taxing is no joke.
Tax his tractor, Tax his mule;

Tell him, Taxing is the rule.

Tax his oil, Tax his gas (again ain't that the truth)
Tax his notes, Tax his cash (oh boy a pattern emerges);
Tax him good and let him know,
That after taxes, he has no dough.

If he hollers, Tax him more;
Tax him till he's good and sore.
Tax his coffin, Tax his grave,
Tax his sod in which he's laid.

Put these words upon his tomb,
"Taxes drove him to his doom."
After he's gone, we won't relax;
We'll still collect inheritance tax.

~*~

A father walks into a market followed by his
ten-year old son. The boy is spinning a 25-cent piece in
the air and catching it between his teeth. As they walk
through the market, someone bumps into the boy at
just the wrong moment and the coin goes straight into
his mouth and lodges in his throat. He immediately
starts choking and going blue in the face and Dad starts
panicking, shouting and screaming for help.

A middle-aged, fairly unnoticeable man in a
gray suit is sitting at a coffee bar in the market reading
his newspaper and sipping a cup of coffee. At the
sound of the commotion, he looks up, puts his coffee

cup down on the saucer, neatly folds his newspaper and places it on the counter. He gets from his seat and makes his unhurried way across the market.

Reaching the boy, the man carefully reaches around the boy's stomach and squeezes forcefully. After a few seconds, the boy convulses violently and coughs up the quarter, which the man catches in his free hand. Releasing the boy, the man hands the coin to the father and walks back to his seat in the coffee bar without saying a word.

As soon as he is sure that his son has suffered no lasting ill effects, the father rushes over to the man and starts effusively thanking him saying, "I've never seen anybody do anything like that before! It was fantastic! Are you a doctor>"

"Oh, good heavens, no," the man replies, "I work for the Internal Revenue Service."

~*~

And, finally:

Sure, you can laugh and smile now. Laugh and have yourself a great time. But just remember. It's **YOUR** money that they are having such a grand time spending.

~Bill Jackson, professional tax cheat~

1854276

Made in the USA